EUTHANASIA: A LICENCE TO KILL?

There is a real urgency around this subject in the UK at the moment. Anthony Smith addresses it with both intellectual clarity and the authority of pastoral experience.

Rowan Williams, Archbishop of Canterbury

Anthony Smith's book covers the complexities of euthanasia and related topics with tremendous clarity. The wealth of his experience brings us stories that are both harrowing and uplifting. We share the burdens of the decision-making process; our hearts go out to carers, family members and patients, and we finally come to a new trust in God's purpose for us all, whatever the situation.

Lyndon Bowring, Chairman of CARE

With pressure in Parliament to legalise physician assisted suicide, Christians urgently need to be up-to-speed. This clear, concise yet comprehensive book is bang up-to-date and its narratives illuminate the biblical arguments that mean we must never give doctors a licence to kill.

Dr Andrew Fergusson
Chairman of the former HOPE,
Healthcare Opposed to Euthanasia

Euthanasia: A Licence to Kill?

ANTHONY M. SMITH

KINGSWAY PUBLICATIONS
EASTBOURNE

ISBN–10: 1 84291 249 6
ISBN–13: 978–1–842912–49–2

KINGSWAY COMMUNICATIONS LTD
Lottbridge Drove, Eastbourne BN23 6NT, England.
Email: books@kingsway.co.uk
Printed in Canada

Contents

Foreword

Whether or not terminally ill people should be allowed to have their lives terminated and, if so, how and by whom, is a question that is being pressed in countries around the world. A few, such as the Netherlands, Belgium and the state of Oregon in the USA, have decided in the affirmative and have legalised either euthanasia or physician-assisted suicide. Elsewhere there is continuing media interest in the often heart-rending situations of individual patients who are asking why they cannot also have their lives ended, in order to relieve their suffering. Instinctively many people feel that such requests are justified and that their government should indeed permit doctors to end the lives of those patients whose suffering has become unbearable.

That such a change in the law would be the right course of action is not as clear as it might seem at first. Dr Smith is well-equipped to explore and clarify the issues involved, having spent many years as a hospice doctor caring for just the sort of people for whose benefit the introduction of euthanasia is being proposed. The Christian reader will find relevant biblical and church teaching explained in this book – as well as a look at the views of the other major faiths.

However, it is important to avoid giving rise to the charge that objection to a change in the law stems from religious bigotry. In fact there are real grounds for fearing that the introduction of euthanasia would disadvantage the frailest and most vulnerable people in our communities, and Dr Smith explains clearly why this is so without shirking from the 'hard cases'.

For instance, a great deal of debate centres on the question of the 'slippery slope'. In other words, would the introduction of euthanasia for a small, select group lead in the future to its application to more and more people whose situations might be different? Proponents of euthanasia say that adequate safeguards can be built into the law, but opponents doubt that safeguards can be so secure in practice. They also point out that once euthanasia has been made available in law this means that it is now considered by the nation to be a benefit. The idea that death could be a benefit to some of its citizens is an extraordinary shift in public morality for any country. But once that shift has occurred it means that euthanasia would have to be looked at in an entirely new way.

It is the responsibility of governments to make sure that benefits of whatever kind are widely distributed among the people who need them. Suffering is certainly not confined to terminally ill people nor to those who are able to ask for euthanasia themselves. Therefore it would become immoral not to proceed down the slippery slope, and there are signs that this is being recognised in those countries where euthanasia is already legal. Over time the attitudes of society to its ill and disabled members and its duty to care for them could not fail to be influenced profoundly by this process in a way that would be difficult if not impossible to reverse.

Dr Smith sets his discussion in a Christian context but takes the reader into the practical considerations that face different kinds of patients and their carers, both professional and lay, and explains the potential consequences of euthanasia and what the alternatives are. The Christian reader will find this book a thoughtful, clear and kindly approach to understanding a change that would not only affect our society as a whole but also, in very practical ways, the lives of all of us and those whom we love.

Dr Nigel Sykes
Medical Director, St Christopher's Hospice, London

Preface

At the very beginning of this book I want to thank people who have stimulated, encouraged and helped in its development. It was written for Kingsway, and especially for a staff member whose family had to face some of the issues explored. I hope this book will help them know that they came to the right decision. Which introduces the fact that it is written from the standpoint of people's experiences rather than being an academic treatise.

It is also written for St Columba's Fellowship (or St C.F. as we affectionately know the fellowship), and in memory of Prue Dufour – or Prue Clench as we used to know her – the lady with the encouraging smile, the prodigious memory and with so much love for the Lord, her patients and her many 'friends'!

Prue had been a district nurse in Bath. She had seen St Christopher's Hospice opened in London by that other inspirational lady, Cicely Saunders. Prue believed that Bath's patients, too, needed hospice care. So in 1977 she left her position as a staff nurse in the radiotherapy department of the Royal United Hospital to set up the Dorothy House Foundation. She became its first domiciliary nurse and a year later sold her own house for conversion into Bath's own hospice. But Prue's influence, like that of Dame Cicely in south London, extended far wider. Through her other creation, St C.F., she kept in touch with nurses, doctors, chaplains, therapists and many other professionals – and *people* – worldwide. She travelled extensively, speaking at seminars and conferences from the Far East to Jamaica and the United States, encouraging people in the hospice move-ment. Thank you, Prue. And thank you, Lord, for giving us people like her – inspirers and encouragers of others.

It is also written in memory of many patients and carers, some of whom feature in these pages. Where possible I have obtained permission of the people or of their relatives to refer to them. Where that has not been possible I have altered names and some of the circumstances in order to preserve the dignity of their memories: I hope they and you will forgive that. But thank you to them for their help in drawing these threads together.

I am indebted to my brother Geoffrey, and to Dr Ben Zylicz of the Hospice in the Weald, for reading the draft and for comments and encouragement. I have benefited from many who have written their own reports, papers and com-mentaries, some of whom I have referred to in the text. For the chapter on the experience abroad I am particularly indebted to the authors of the Report of the Select Com-mittee of the House of Lords on the Assisted Dying for the Terminally Ill Bill, the Billet d'Etat of the Policy Council of the States of the Island of Guernsey, and the reports pub-lished by various Dutch authors in the *New England Journal of Medicine* of 28 November 1996 and the *Lancet* of 2 August 2003, as well as to writers from different religious convictions, each of which will be fully referenced at the end of the book.

Finally, I want to thank my wife Sheila for her patience with my preoccupation during the last six months, and for being left to her own devices during the most recent 'holiday' (which enabled me to finish the writing) and for her unfailing encouragement. Above all, I thank her for her shared love for the Lord Jesus who, beyond all others, has kept my eyes on the goal.

May this book be a help to those Christians, for whom, ultimately, it is written, who are facing the issue of an incurable illness, their own or their loved one's, and who seek relief and release! May you, too, know the sustaining and comforting peace of God, which passes all understanding, and which many have experienced as they draw near to the opened gates of Life!

1

Jim's Story

How could Jim tell them?

The nurses were so kind. They attended to his every need, and that wasn't easy when words wouldn't come. The food had always been good, but it was less appetising mushed up – though they did give him different piles of mush to help him know it was meat, gravy and three veg. He could do without visitors; there was always plenty going on around him, and he had lots of friends among the others. Yes, he'd always wanted to stay on the ward because of the folk around – 'being where the action was', as one of his friends used to say.

But the truth was that life . . . well, to be truthful . . . life had lost its meaning. Yes, that was the heart of it; life wasn't worth living.

Jim had noticed a year or so earlier that he was becoming unsteady when he walked. Then his hands seemed to be clumsier and his voice began to get weaker. He'd gone to his doctor and after a series of visits he had been referred to the specialist at King's College Hospital. There he'd had lots of tests and they had explained to him that he had developed motor neurone disease, a progressive and incurable disease of the nervous system affecting the parts of the brain controlling muscle activity. 'Sometimes,' they had said, 'it affects only the limbs, and then it may progress quite slowly, but when it affects the voice or swallowing it often goes faster.'

And that was how it had been. Now here he was in the local hospice, with little movement in arms or legs and no voice at all. Even his neck was weak and needed support. At least his swallowing had not been affected – yet!

Jim was in a four-bedded bay with an interesting view, and he enjoyed the other patients being around. He had declined the offer of a single room some weeks earlier – he preferred the company. He knew the staff now and they were OK! But he had to be fed; he had to be bathed or washed; he had to be shaved and have his hair done; toilet arrangements – well. . .! And now his speech had gone completely and he had to make himself understood with eye movements and a letter-board which the nurses held. They were very patient, but this was no life.

Jim decided simply to refuse food and fluids. He would end the problem. The staff understood. Initially they tried to persuade him, but then they accepted he had made up his mind, and simply offered food at each meal and accepted his refusal. It lasted a couple of days and then he accepted drinks again. But the nurses and doctors were worried about Jim. After discussion, a couple of staff whom he trusted came and sat with him. What could they do to make life more worthwhile? They made various suggestions but it was evident they were not on the right track.

Jim tackled the letter-board – 'I w-a-n-t a r-o-o-m o-n m-y o-w-n.'

Was that wise? Jim could do nothing to call for help, not even ring the bell on the bed. Would he be safe? But if that was what would make life a little easier, they'd do all they could to make it possible. So he went into the single room, a bell was rigged up so that if he moved his head the slightest bit it would ring, and the nurses looked in as often as was possible.

Some weeks later there was a cold going round and somehow Jim caught it. If it went onto his chest that could easily be the end. Yes, 'easily', we thought, 'in every sense of that word.' Only a few weeks ago Jim had tried to starve himself; now if he could go easily would that not be best for him? At the ward meeting the doctors said that it would be perfectly proper to treat Jim with medications to keep him comfortable and to prevent any distress, but in view of his recent attempt to starve himself we would not offer antibiotics. The ward nurses were unhappy with that.

'Why not ask him?' they said.

So one of the doctors and one of the nurses went to see Jim. The letter-board came out again, and we waited while Jim laboriously spelled out: 'I w-a-n-t t-h-e a-n-t-i-b-i-o-t-i-c-s.' Life had regained its value!

Jim's story raises a number of matters that we shall want to explore in the chapters of this book. First, it raises the matter of dignity in dying. Was dignity in fact behind Jim's unhappiness? We shall need to ask about what is involved in dignity. The fact is that Jim's going into the single room meant that feeding, washing, toilet and so on could be done more privately than behind screens. Is that important? The issue of dignity is going to underpin all that we talk about in this book.

Then there is the issue of suicide and euthanasia. Jim's is not a story about euthanasia, but about the value of life and about what can make death seem preferable to a very limited life, coping with disability, or weakness, or pain, or simply with age. We shall need to look at definitions of suicide, assisted suicide and euthanasia, and try to clarify for ourselves the issues, the pros and cons, and whether there is any definitive guidance to be found. That will occupy our first four chapters; after all, this is a book about the euthanasia issue. We shall need to see the very clear and obvious case for euthanasia, and we will try to do that without prejudice. We need also to see the case against euthanasia, and, because this book has been written with Christian considerations in mind, we shall see what guidance we can gain from the Bible.

For many of us, the central question is what we understand about suffering. Jim's suffering is obvious enough . . . isn't it? And yet weeks after his attempted suicide and when he was even weaker and so very disabled, life had regained value enough for him to request the antibiotics. And when it was the doctors who advised to refrain from antibiotics, do we catch a glimpse of someone else's suffering? We will need to enquire about people's suffering about others, or on behalf of others.

We certainly need to ask whether not starting treatment and withdrawal of treatment are legally and morally acceptable. Was it right even to consider not giving Jim antibiotics? And if so, when is that appropriate? Suppose Jim had written an 'advance directive' or 'living will' some two years earlier, when he was in excellent health, stating that he would or would not want treatment at all if he was severely disabled; would the medical and nursing staff have altered their actions? So we look at these issues in Chapters 8 to 10. We hear a lot about 'autonomy' these days: my right to make my own decisions. It is regarded as one of the pillars of ethical practice, and we will explore its implications – and ask the question, 'Whose autonomy?' The nurses expressed it eloquently when they insisted, 'Ask him.'

The account raises the issue of the place of care. Jim was in a hospice, and the question of whether he could be discharged to a long-stay nursing home was raised. Or could he go home? No, he was on his own at home, having had a divorce some years earlier. Home on his own was simply not possible, however effective the adaptations – and there are many very ingenious adaptations available for disabled people these days. Should he be sent back to the acute hospital, or why not a nursing home transfer?

We must look at the question of alternatives for people: alternatives in the matter of place of care, and also in the matter of methods of treatment. For Jim, it was an enormous relief that he could spend his last months in the hospice, and that was never in doubt; although the hospice staff had to ask whether it was appropriate for him to occupy a hospice bed long term when others could not get into the hospice. Was his need really specialist palliative care, as they call it, or could his care have been managed elsewhere in his particular community? And what would he want? Autonomy again!

Ultimately Jim raises the importance of hope. Hope is

vital to all of us, and one of the commonest reasons for people's asking for euthanasia is not pain but despair. We will look at the matter of despair and hope as we come to the conclusion of our exploration together, and will dwell for a while on the Christian hope which is such a powerful strength to the believer.

There are some issues that Jim does not raise for us, but that we shall need to think about as well. What about legal considerations? What is the law in the matter of euthanasia, and how might a change in the law affect our relationships with our doctors and our places of care? What about the law and advance directives? What can we request and what matters are off-limits, as it were?

Then we shall need to enquire about experience of countries where euthanasia has been decriminalised if not legalised. What has the benefit of their experience taught us?

And the questions of faith, spirituality and religious practice did not surface in Jim's story. These, too, are important questions for us, and should influence our attitude to despair and hope, to death and life. We shall spend time on these matters in regard to euthanasia, but they will also prove to be relevant to other parts of our exploration.

But what happened to Jim in the end?

Jim had a mild bout with his cold, and, whether because of the antibiotics or not, his chest was not affected. He stayed in the single room, was cared for effectively – I dare to say, lovingly – by the ward staff, doctors, nurses, social workers and chaplain, over a further month or so, and then very peacefully passed into unconsciousness and died within 24 hours. He had been on the ward for some four or more months, and his death left a big gap in the hearts of many staff. We remember Jim with affection.

We may ask whether his last very disabled months were simply suffering, or dignified dying. And in the end each reader will have to make up her or his own mind.

2

A Personal Dilemma

We were worried about Mother. She was nearly 90 years old, and had a combination of the chronic problems that characterise a body that is wearing out. That meant she had to get up several times a night, and *that* meant that Dad had to get up too. By day, as well, she had to visit the loo many times – and Dad had to be there to help her. He was in his 80s, had high blood pressure and had had a blackout or two. Add to this that Mum's memory was not what it used to be – and that is an understatement. She had actually got lost on her way to the letterbox at the end of the road, and a neighbour had helped her back home, fortunately.

But Mother did understand what was going on. She and Dad were both convinced Christians, committed to their faith in life and behaviour, and both spent time in prayer. Mother understood what failing memory and declining strength meant; and in her case, it meant being increasingly dependent on Dad and increasingly frustrated by her disabilities.

We were living 200 miles away, but visited whenever

possible, and always enjoyed the opportunities to share our lives and experiences. Mother was always on top form with us, although we could see the deterioration in her health. One morning she took the opportunity of our being just the two together to ask the question she had been pondering for weeks (or months perhaps): 'Couldn't I have euthanasia, dear?'

How should I, a practising doctor, and Mother's son, reply?

What is euthanasia?

Properly translated, eu-thanasia is simply 'good dying' (from the Greek eu = good, and thanatos = death). Who would not want a good death? And what son would not want a good death for his mother?

However, the word has been adopted to mean mercy-killing, and is defined as 'the termination of life of a person, by act or omission, when that life is deemed to be no longer worth living'. Killing a person is illegal in almost all countries except in circumstances of war or, in some countries, as a punishment for heinous crimes. What might make it acceptable to take the life of frail, disabled or dependent people in a civilised society?

First, let us explore three other definitions and to do that we will look at three imaginary situations.

'Tom' has been told he has incurable cancer. He asks for euthanasia because of his pain and intolerable suffering.

'Bill' was involved in a major road accident some weeks earlier. He is paralysed from the neck down and has been deeply unconscious ever since the accident. His parents have asked the doctors to provide euthanasia in view of the very poor outlook.

'Auntie Maud' has been in a nursing home for years with advancing dementia. It is incurable, and she sits in the home looking lost and hopeless most of the time. Her relatives ask the doctors to arrange euthanasia for her since her suffering is so great and the future hopeless.

For the purposes of our argument we have reason to believe all three are committed Christians, so that their life hereafter is not an issue.

In Tom's case, to acquiesce would be *voluntary euthanasia*, since Tom has requested it for himself. He is alert and in his right mind; he knows where he is and what he is about. He could make a rational request: he is 'competent' to make this request.

Response to Bill's parents' request would be to perform *non-voluntary euthanasia*, for Bill himself has had no opportunity or possibility of being involved in the request, as he has been unconscious all along.

On the other hand, to respond to Auntie Maud's relatives' request would be to provide *involuntary euthanasia*, for Maud has not requested euthanasia herself although she could do so in her more lucid periods, or could have indicated that that is what she would want under such circumstances. She hasn't.

It is important to distinguish these three types of euthanasia, and to note that involuntary and non-voluntary euthanasia are not responses to requests by the candidate; other people are making decisions from what they regard as the candidate's best interests.

Bill's case allows us to make two further distinctions.

Supposing it were legal to perform euthanasia and that we wished to do what his parents wanted, we could do so actively by injecting a suitable chemical into one of his veins and causing his heart to stop; that would be *active euthanasia*. Alternatively, we could decide to withdraw all useful treatment and allow Bill to die, and that would be *passive euthanasia* – but we must note that the intention of both these methods is to cause Bill's death.

This is important because it might be perfectly good medicine to withdraw treatment from Bill that was futile or burdensome, and this would not be euthanasia since it was not the *intention* to cause death. In practice the terms active and passive euthanasia are not very helpful, since the purpose and effect of each is to kill the patient.

Arguments for euthanasia

Our account has already given some of the reasons advanced for the practice of euthanasia. Broadly, the arguments can be drawn together under four headings.

Compassion or need

Mother's appeal expressed a need she was feeling, and it appealed to her son's compassionate feelings for his mother. Patients sometimes tell us of severe pain or other symptoms, like breathlessness or nausea, which are overwhelming. They, or more often their relatives, say, 'You would not let a dog suffer like this. If a farmer had an animal suffering as he or she is, he would have had it put down. Why not let her or him (or me) die?'

Surprisingly perhaps, this argument is infrequent even in

hospice practice, largely because of the improvement in the relief of distressing symptoms available nowadays, with better medicines and more concentration on effective communication.

Nevertheless, it is perfectly true that while medical and nursing staff and their colleagues work hard to relieve symptoms, they cannot always get rid of them completely. Indeed, sometimes even the caring doctor or nurse feels that the kind thing would be to release the patient from the distress by easing their life away.

A doctor's response to a request for euthanasia

Mrs Lilian Boyes was an elderly lady who, in 1991, had suffered from rheumatoid arthritis for some years. She was a patient of Dr Nigel Cox, a rheumatologist, who had looked after her caringly. Now an in-patient on a hospital ward because of her advanced and very painful condition, she was crying 'like a dog' with her pain. She refused various medications and over some days pleaded repeatedly for tablets or an injection to end her life. Dr Cox attempted to control her pain with rising doses of a strong painkiller, diamorphine. One day he visited her on the ward. An injection of diamorphine failed to control the pain and he went to the drug cupboard, selected an ampoule of a chemical solution which he injected into Mrs Boyes' vein and shortly afterwards Mrs Boyes died. Dr Cox then wrote out a death certificate for Mrs Boyes and recorded his action and his reasons in her hospital notes.

Mrs Boyes' body was cremated.

The ward sister returned from leave and was surprised not to find Mrs Boyes. She enquired after her and then read the hospital notes which were available to her. The chemical concerned is not a painkiller but, given in adequate dose through a vein, would cause the heart to stop. The ward sister reported Dr Cox's action to the hospital authorities. Dr Cox was arrested and tried. Because the body had been cremated and it could not be proved that Mrs Boyes had died as a direct result of the injection (she might have sustained a coincidental heart attack, for example), Dr Cox was found not guilty of murder but was convicted of attempted murder and was given a suspended prison sentence of one year. Then the General Medical Council found him unfit to practise until he had received a course of training in palliative medicine.

Pain is a problem for many cancer patients. One of my patients told me that when he heard that he had cancer he thought it meant: 'Pain and more pain until one day I explode from my pain.' Asked if he had pain, he replied, 'Not yet.' His relief when told that cancer did not necessarily mean pain, and that it was usually controllable, was powerful! However, it is not only cancer that leads to pain: the account of Mrs Boyes and the rheumatologist Dr Cox (described in the box above) instances the pain she experienced from arthritis. While it is true that most pain can be removed or at least controlled to a very large degree, we must acknowledge that some pain is very difficult to relieve completely. In other cases the amount of medication its relief requires may be unacceptable to the patient: 'Do I really have to take all these pills for the rest of my life, doctor?' And sadly not all doctors are skilled in relieving pain, or willing to seek help from colleagues. The result is that recent surveys have indicated that some, perhaps many, people continue to suffer pain needlessly in their advanced illness.

More intractable still is the feeling of despair that may grip people when told of an incurable illness and when they feel there is no hope. Hope is such an important matter that we shall devote a whole chapter to the subject. At this stage it is important to note that requests for euthanasia today are much more likely to be based on a feeling of despair than because of unrelieved physical symptoms. We may also note that the widespread absence of belief in God has led to a sense of pointlessness in both suffering and a life limited in length or quality.

Of course, this sense of despair is often part of a depressive reaction. Depression is an important symptom and it is treatable. Response to treatment is slow, and we need to recognise the occurrence of depression early and provide active treatment for it with counselling or psychological support and with medication.

When a person's distress or the despair of the relatives is unrelieved, a compassionate response would seem to be the legalising of euthanasia.

Autonomy

In medical matters there has been a major shift in our way of thinking in Britain and the Western world. It is not long ago that doctor knew what was best for us. 'Doctor says' – and we followed the recommendation.

Not so today. We expect to question, to seek advice from the Internet and other sources, and to make up our own minds as to what we will take or agree to. Of course, this is not invariable, and there are still a lot of people around who say, 'I prefer to leave these sorts of things to you, Doctor. I'll do what you advise, and don't worry me with the details.'

Even so, we make our own decisions as to what we leave to the doctor, and what we will decide about – and when. All this is a reflection of what is called 'exercising our autonomy': my right to decide what I want. Gone is the old paternalism of the all-wise doctor! And why should we not make up our own minds when we can seek our own advice – or follow the latest adverts!

Increasingly through the twentieth century and into the twenty-first, we are able to control our lives, and to have what we desire. The credit boom is evidence of this pervading spirit of 'It's what I want; why shouldn't I have it or do it?' In the realm of rights we talk about our autonomy, our individual interest. So with our health, we expect effective treatment when we want it.

And if we cannot be cured, then we ought to be able to be relieved of our suffering when we want, too, oughtn't we?

That was the basis of Mrs Diane Pretty's plea in 2004. Mrs Pretty had developed motor neurone disease and was confined to bed or a wheelchair. The condition was deteriorating. Her husband cared for her in every way, but now she wanted to have the way clear for her to have euthanasia if and when she wished. She appealed to the authorities that if her husband performed euthanasia for her he should not be prosecuted. This was, she averred, her right under the European human rights legislation. The case was pursued through the British courts up to the House of Lords, and then an appeal was made to the European Court of Human Rights.

She argued that the human rights legislation supported a right to life for everyone. Therefore there must be an equal right to have that life terminated when the owner wished, a 'Right to Die'. The Courts consistently disagreed and the Court of Human Rights did not support her appeal. Mrs Pretty actually died from her illness shortly after these actions.

But the argument from autonomy feels very strong. Even if there is no Right to Die in law, many people feel that they should be able to request the end when they want it, particularly if they are found to be suffering from an incurable and progressive illness. The dying could then be planned for the convenience of the relatives, and the patient could perhaps be spared the worst of any unpleasant symptoms at the end of the dying period.

Economics

A further reason to demand euthanasia arises from personal, family and community economics. It may be expensive for a person to be supported through a long period of frailty and suffering. It will very likely be demanding on the family, financially and emotionally, to support a loved one through such a period. And it is expensive for the state to provide medical and social care for people whose lives are not thought to be worth living.

We might cite 'Dorothy' as an example. Dorothy was in

many ways the most disabled person on the hospice ward. She had advanced breast cancer, which had not responded to the various treatments she had had – and I am talking about 20 years or so ago. She had sustained a number of bone fractures, some of which had mended with resultant deformity, and others had not mended fully. She needed to remain on traction in bed to keep her out of pain. However, she was invariably cheerful and interested in other people, but the strain of life seemed to be telling – and not least on her closest relative.

This relative was a senior nurse in a busy intensive-care ward of a city hospital, where the staff were daily facing difficult and often harrowing decisions. Every day after work she would come to spend time with Dorothy. But the journey and the daily visits were wearing. We could see the strain it was to her, and we admired her for her costly commitment. So when she asked how much longer it would go on, and surely we would not need to treat any future chest infection with antibiotics, we understood what she was saying, even though we might not agree.

In the event we were able to recommend that our friend need not visit every day, but could entrust Dorothy to the staff and her many other friends. Dorothy continued to enjoy her life on the ward and ultimately died very peacefully four months later. Afterwards this same relative spoke warmly of the happy months that Dorothy had spent in the hospice. Nevertheless, the months had obviously been costly emotionally and financially to her, and the months of care had been costly to the hospice community.

Dorothy's example gives us an insight into the emotional cost of caring for someone. The financial cost to the community of providing care for a frail person at home is also considerable. Adaptations may be needed to the home – safety rails, a stair-lift, an adapted bathroom with special aids for bath or shower; some will need two or more visits each day from the district nurses; someone to clean, shop, perhaps cook or provide meals; carers to visit twice a day to help wash and dress the person and to get them back to bed; and so on. That sort of support may enable people to continue in their own home for months or years – at a cost to the community.

Even more costly is prolonged residential-home or nursing-home care for elderly and mentally disabled people suffering from conditions that are not fatal but demand continuing care.

In some countries where hospital care is not free at the point of need, the cost to people of having a family member in hospital for a significant period may be crippling. When it is evident that such a hospital stay cannot result in a cure, the family – with or without involvement of the sick person – may want to consider other options. 'Doesn't it make sense,' they may ask, 'to allow euthanasia for such as wish it?'

To provide control of practice

'And doesn't it happen anyway, here in the United Kingdom?'

Of course it's illegal, but anonymous surveys of British doctors since 1998 have reported that some individual doctors have, in all kindness, helped some of their patients to die. Very few cases indeed have come before the courts, and we have already referred to Dr Cox and Mrs Boyes;

Dr Moor's case will be discussed in Chapter 4, but he was one who declared he had shortened a life, only to claim in court – and have accepted – that the treatment he had given was to relieve pain. Indeed, this is often the question: Was the intention of the medication to relieve pain or distress, or to terminate life? The former is totally legal, even if, coincidentally, it might shorten life.

Official medical circles claim that they have no evidence of the practice of euthanasia in the UK, but individual doctors still record that they have helped people to die. If this is happening in covert fashion, some people argue that it would be better to make it legal with strict controls, and thus be able to regulate any such practice.

What, we might ask, has happened in countries where euthanasia has been legalised? Is there any evidence that the practice has been effectively controlled, and that illegal practice has disappeared? Or does practice outside the law still occur?

3

Euthanasia in Europe and Elsewhere

How are countries outside the United Kingdom dealing with the question of requests for euthanasia?

In general it is true to say that euthanasia is viewed as murder and is proscribed in almost all countries. The exceptions are the Netherlands, Belgium, Switzerland, and the State of Oregon in the United States of America.[1,2] The Northern Territories of Australia passed a law legalising euthanasia in 1995, but it was overturned by the Australian Federal Government two years later.[2] The biggest example of the practice of euthanasia being legalised was in Germany in the 1930s and 40s, but there the practice has been outlawed ever since.

As in the United Kingdom, many countries have societies actively promoting the concept of euthanasia and seeking to have laws enacted accordingly. Bills have been introduced in parliament in other American states, in Canada, New Zealand and the United Kingdom, but have not been approved. And in some other countries cases have come before the courts, and sympathetic judgments have been given, but no change in the laws has resulted. Proposals have also been discussed at the Council of Europe and at the United Nations, but without their being agreed.

In this chapter we will explore the experience in the countries where euthanasia has been legalised and then note the attitude of some of the major world religions.

The Netherlands[1,2,5]

Between 1973 and 1990, Dutch courts had had to adjudicate on a number of cases of euthanasia by doctors who gave 'force majeur' or 'necessity' as a reason for their action. Their patients had been suffering excessively and could not be relieved medically; they had been demanding medical termination of life as part of their medical treatment and the doctor was said to have felt trapped between an honest and honourable request on the one hand and, on the other, something that was prohibited by law. He had felt obliged to concur. The criminal and supreme courts had generally accepted this defence and 'in certain circumstances you are acquitted. It is not that it is not criminal, it is just that you don't go to prison for it.'

At this time there were practically no hospices in the Netherlands and the practice of palliative care was very poorly developed in the country. We shall see that this situation has changed considerably since.

A careful review of end-of-life decision-making practice was undertaken in 1990, using a very wide survey of what doctors said they had done over the previous year.[3] Replies were kept strictly anonymous and assurance was given that no legal action would follow from the answers. It became apparent that some 39% of deaths in the country were preceded by a medical decision that probably or certainly hastened the death. So in 1991 the circumstances under which such cases would be acquitted were specified, so that the practice could be controlled. If these conditions were observed the cases would not be brought before the courts. Five conditions were enunciated:

1. The patient must consider his or her suffering unbearable and hopeless.
2. The patient's wish to die must be well considered and persistent.
3. The request must be voluntary.
4. The physician must consult at least one other physician.
5. The physician may not ascribe the death to natural causes and must keep records.

The act would be conducted by a physician and must subsequently be notified to the coroner as a case of physician-assisted death. The procedure was agreed and brought into use in 1991, and enacted legally in 1994.

Further careful, anonymised studies into the practice were undertaken in 1995 and 2001 and were published.[4] In 2002 the law was amended to allow the practice of euthanasia to become legal, but did not significantly alter the conditions under which the physician might perform it.

You will see that by definition euthanasia in the Netherlands is what we have described as voluntary euthanasia. It does include physician-assisted suicide where the physician prescribes a lethal potion which the patient then self-administers. But if the patient did not express the wish for euthanasia, mercy-killing remained murder; so that what we have described as involuntary and non-voluntary euthanasia is still against the law.

So what of the practice? The studies in 1995 and 2001 found that only about half the cases of euthanasia were actually being reported. Of a total of 129,000 deaths in 1992, 3,000 had been by euthanasia, and this proportion remained more or less constant over the next ten years. But there was also a constant figure of 1% of physician-assisted deaths (over 1,080 per year) where there had been no expression of wish for it by the patient. These included people who were in a coma or mentally confused, and late in their terminal illness, but might also have included congenitally deformed infants. For the purpose of Dutch law these could not be classified as euthanasia as there was not (and could not be) a request from the patient. But they continued to happen after legalisation of euthanasia, although they continued not to be reported as euthanasia, and are, of course, still illegal.

Another difficulty (perhaps for outside observers) has been the question of what constitutes unbearable and hopeless suffering. You will notice that Dutch law does not codify the medical conditions that can lead to these requests. Periodically euthanasia has been practised for people who were not terminally ill but were suffering from depression. Recently, someone asked for euthanasia because he was 'tired of life'.

We said that there was very little palliative care in the Netherlands in 1990. The situation has changed greatly since, partly at least as a consequence of the euthanasia legislation and the international scrutiny that it has provoked.

Funding for palliative care was increased for a period of some five years from the late 1990s, and resulted in the opening of new palliative care units, sometimes in institutions which had been providing nursing care. Unfortunately, it is reported that the increase has been in quantity rather than in quality of care, so that requests for euthanasia still stem from inadequate control of symptoms.

Palliative care is not a specialty in the Netherlands, and so hospitals remain largely devoid of input from palliative care specialists.

The American State of Oregon[1]

The State of Oregon passed its Death With Dignity Act in 1994 as a Citizens' Initiative, meaning that it was proposed by individuals and was voted on by the state electorate. Its application was delayed for a further three years but it was then ratified and has been in action since 1997.

The Act allows a physician to prescribe a lethal dose of medication for use by the patient. The patient must have reached the age of majority and be terminally ill. This is defined as having a life expectancy of less than six months. He is required to have made two written requests for such a prescription separated by at least 15 days. Once issued with such a prescription, the patient may decide to have it dispensed or to keep it as a sort of insurance policy against such a time when he feels the need has arisen. There is careful monitoring of the use of the Act, although such deaths are not recorded as suicide and are not investigated.

The Oregon Department of Human Services is required to record the number of lethal prescriptions issued and the number actually used. They report to the Oregon Board of Health Examiners, which is the regulatory body for the medical profession in the state. From 1997 to 2003, 265 prescriptions had been issued and 117 people had chosen to use them. In 2003, this amounted to 42 out of 30,000 deaths. You can see that this is a very much smaller proportion than under the Dutch system of euthanasia.

A limited number of doctors are willing to participate in this service, and the profession is divided into those doctors who see the Act as a necessary and appropriate part of their medical practice, those who will never prescribe in this way because of conscience, and a large number who are undecided but who will assess any request at the time. Some people are concerned that prescriptions issued may be dispensed but then the person may decide simply to keep the medicine in a cupboard and not use it. There is no check on what happens to the lethal dose of medication, which may stay in the community.

Hospice services are widely available in the States. These services differ from those in the UK as they are largely home-care services, and once a patient is registered with the hospice, return to the acute health services is no longer possible, even for a comparatively basic investigation, because of funding under the American Medicare system.

We shall be referring to this provision further in the chapter on suicide and assisted suicide (Chapter 7).

Belgium[1]

Belgium legalised euthanasia in 2002. This followed some large-scale research which showed that more than one in ten deaths in the country were by euthanasia, although it was not legal, and that most of these deaths were without a request from the patient. It was hoped that regulating the practice would protect vulnerable people from abuse. The provisions also included raising awareness of palliative care.

The Belgian Act defines euthanasia as 'intentionally terminating life by someone other than the person concerned at the latter's request'. In this way it legalises (voluntary) euthanasia but not physician-assisted suicide.

The conditions are:

- that the patient has achieved the age of majority
- that the patient is in a futile medical condition of constant and unbearable physical or mental suffering that cannot be alleviated
- that the physician has had several conversations with the patient over a reasonable period of time and has assured himself of the durable nature of the request
- that a second opinion from another doctor has been obtained
- that at least a month must have elapsed between the patient's request and the act of euthanasia

An act of euthanasia has then to be reported to the Federal Control and Evaluation Commission, which either confirms the doctor's immunity from prosecution (on the grounds of the paperwork), or refers the case to the public prosecutor.

In the first 15 months following this Act 259 cases of euthanasia were recorded, 80% being in Dutch-speaking Flanders which has 60% of Belgium's population, and only 20% in French-speaking Wallonia. In the following year 347 cases were reported out of a total of about 56,000 deaths in the country. However, reporting is certainly far from complete.

The same law declared that every person in Belgium should have access to proper palliative care, and that patients requesting euthanasia should be made aware of this option.

It is too early to know what effect this law will have on the practice of euthanasia in Belgium.

Switzerland[1,2]

In Switzerland the situation is very different. Assisted suicide and euthanasia are illegal in Switzerland, but since 1937 the Swiss Penal Code exempts from penalty people who assist with someone's suicide from entirely honourable motives – such as bringing an end to suffering – though never if they assist for selfish reasons. It does not require the involvement of a physician or that the person is terminally ill. Where use of a lethal medication is involved a doctor's prescription is needed under the regulations for control of dangerous drugs, not because of a view that a doctor should be involved in assistance with suicide.

The majority of assisted suicides that occur in Switzerland are not supervised by a doctor. There are a number of voluntary suicide organisations in the country, the largest of which is EXIT, which has a membership of about 50,000 and caters for the German- and Italian-speaking regions. A second society, AMD, caters for the French-speaking areas. A breakaway group from EXIT called DIGNITAS has a membership of some 4,500 and caters for the foreign nationals entering the country for assistance with suicide as well as for nationals. There are other smaller groups, too. These groups offer medical examinations and facilities for suicide to take place.

More recently the Swiss Academy of Medical Sciences has drawn up a set of medical ethical principles for end-of-life care. These state that physician-assisted suicide is not a part of medical practice, but agree that while the doctor's role is to alleviate symptoms and to support the patient, there may be circumstances in which the patient asks persistently for help in committing suicide. In this dilemma the doctor may either refuse to comply, or may accede provided he is sure that three conditions have been met:

- that the patient's medical condition makes clear that he or she is nearing the end of life
- that alternative possibilities for treatment have been discussed and considered by the patient
- that the patient is capable, free from external pressure and has thought through the decision

So-called 'suicide tourism' began around the year 2000, and became prominent when a Mr Reginald Crew, from England, travelled to Switzerland in 2003 (see box). Of the countries that allow euthanasia or assisted suicide, Switzerland is the only one that does not require that the person be under established medical care from the person assisting.

Reginald Crew

Reginald Crew was a British citizen and a member of the Swiss organisation DIGNITAS. He was 74 years old and had developed motor neurone disease. At the end of

2002 he had lost all use of his arms and his legs, and his neck was becoming weak. His time was spent in a wheelchair or in bed. In January 2003 he travelled to Switzerland with his 71-year-old wife, Win. Within 24 hours of their arrival, he had been given a fatal dose, reportedly of barbiturates, and died.

The circumstances of Mr Crew's decision and the setting for his euthanasia were widely publicised in the United Kingdom through publicity engendered by the Voluntary Euthanasia Society.

Australia: the Northern Territory[2]

The Northern Territory of Australia is a very large area, about the size of France and Germany combined, but has a population of 150,000. In May 1995 the government of the Territory passed an Act legalising voluntary euthanasia for individuals who were terminally ill, were over the age of 18, and who requested euthanasia over a period of at least seven days. The patient had to have had his status confirmed by a second doctor, and to have been seen by a psychiatrist to make sure they were not suffering from a treatable depression. There was provision of a 'cooling-off' period of at least 48 hours before the euthanasia was performed. The action could be done either by the patient or by a medical practitioner and it had to be reported as euthanasia. The provision would apply also to non-residents in the Territory.

There was considerable opposition to the passing of the Act, but it came into force a year later (on 1st July 1996). During the next eight months four people with advanced cancer had their lives terminated under the Act, but it was then overturned by the Federal Government of Australia, on the grounds that the Northern Territory is not a state within Australia.

Religious viewpoints

We should reflect briefly on the attitude to euthanasia of five of the world's religions – Islam, Judaism, Buddhism, Hinduism and Christianity. In no case do all adherents of these religions have totally uniform beliefs and practices, let alone attitudes towards moral and philosophical questions. It will not be possible, therefore, to reflect all shades of opinion here, and we will need to understand this. However, we will try to give an overall view. In doing so I have sought help from a number of papers which are acknowledged in the Notes at the end of the book.

It will come as no surprise that, in principle, all these faiths are opposed to the killing of people. All begin with a strong predisposition to the preserving of life, and yet they also recognise that death is a natural part of human existence. It is in dealing with situations where life is accompanied by severe pain or distress, or where a person is in a coma with no likelihood of recovery but maintained alive by the modern technologies of life support, that differences emerge.

Islam

Islam is the most specific and categorical in its pronunciations. Boldly stated, 'euthanasia has no place in Islam'.

Euthanasia and suicide are viewed as morally equivalent.

The Qur'an teaches people 'not to kill yourself; indeed God is merciful to you' (4:29).

> The prophet Muhammad said, 'In the time before you, a man was wounded. His wounds troubled him so much that he took a knife and cut his wrist and bled to death. Thereupon God said: "My servant hurried in the matter of his life. Therefore he is deprived of the garden [of Paradise]"' (Hadith: Bukhari 8:603). From this quotation, Muslims are forbidden to take their own lives. If out of despair someone took their own life then not only has the individual taken what doesn't belong to him, but significantly the community has also failed in its responsibility to meet the needs of one experiencing a psychological and spiritual void. A Muslim must never give permission to others to take their lives nor must they assist them. In Islamic communities the lives of the old are just as sacred as the young. Death is a time allotted by God. Nor can a person die except by God's leave, the term being fixed as waiting (Qur'an 3:145).

Suffering is not to be endured for its own sake, so far as it can be eased. However, it can be an occasion for spiritual growth – even the manner in which it is endured can have a moral effect on attendants and observers.[6]

'The sanctity of human life is a basic value decreed by God. The Qur'an says: "Take not life which Allah made sacred otherwise than in the course of justice" (Qur'an 6:151 and 17:33).' Patience and endurance are highly regarded and highly rewarded values in Islam: 'Those who patiently preserve will truly receive a reward without measure' (Qur'an 39:10).

According to Islam, each life belongs to the creator and we can neither shorten it nor prolong it. This all implies that euthanasia is prohibited; that we may and should utilise means available to maintain life and to relieve pain and distress; but that we may not remove life support. Further Islamic rules suggest that as long as efforts are sincere and the intentions are to abide by Islamic rules and follow the commands of Allah, no one is held responsible for the results. Ultimately, knowing that every single one will die when Allah wills him to die, Muslims are asked only to do their best, within the Islamic regulations, in any treatment decisions they make.[7]

Judaism

Judaism, both Orthodox and Reform, is equally clear: active euthanasia violates Jewish law.

However, Reform Judaism permits passive euthanasia, where passive euthanasia is defined as when 'the physician withdraws or withholds treatment and the patient is killed *by the disease'*.[8] We have already made a distinction between appropriate withdrawal or withholding of burdensome or futile treatment and passive euthanasia, when we remarked that this term is not very helpful. Here we see something of the confusion produced by the term.

The principle is that every moment of life is God's gift and therefore precious. We must do all we can to relieve suffering and to enhance quality of life, but a poor quality of life is not an excuse for hastening death:

Pain and suffering are part and parcel of the human condition. The choice we face when we are ill is essentially the same choice we confront at every other moment of our lives: to determine what we, human beings in covenant with God, propose to do with the time and the strength available to us on this earth . . . Judaism, for its part, bids us to respond to the challenges of life by *choosing* life, to praise God whether that brings us joy or sorrow. Even in debilitating illness . . . we yet sanctify the Divine name . . . by striving toward nobility of conduct and purpose, by confronting our sufferings with courage. To say this is not to ignore the agony of the dying, but to recognise a fundamental truth: that even when we are dying we have the power to choose how we shall live.[9]

Reform Judaism is clear that it is acceptable to use medication to relieve pain and suffering, even though the increased dosage might hasten a person's death. If the intent is to relieve pain and suffering it is permissible; however 'if it is our intent to end a life, to "put this person out of his or her misery," then the answer is a resounding "no"'.[10]

However, where a patient is dying, there is no absolute requirement to use the whole arsenal of technologies, surgeries, medicines and machines to delay a person's inevitable death. Reform Judaism states: 'There is a long tradition for allowing individuals not only a return to health but also a peaceful death.' And, 'Nothing needs to be done for someone who is clearly and obviously dying and whose death is close. At that stage we may not remove life support systems, but we also need not institute any procedures.'[(9)]

Hinduism

Hinduism, we are told, tends to focus on the consequences of actions rather than the abstract ideas of right and wrong favoured by Western philosophers. The religion teaches a cycle of birth, death and rebirth; a cycle of reincarnation through many lives (not necessarily all human). One should aim at attaining liberation from this cycle by the excellence of one's 'karma': the balance of the consequence of good and bad actions in this and previous lives. One of the further principles of Hinduism is 'ahimsa': non-violence; not causing violence or harm to others. Hindus are required to live according to their moral duties and responsibilities – their 'dharma' – and this requires taking care of older members of their community.

All this is of obvious relevance to the issue of euthanasia, but it does not all point in the same direction!

To perform euthanasia for a person requesting it would violate the principle of ahimsa (doing no harm), and would affect the doer's dharma: their responsibility for the care of elderly or needy members of the community. Equally, it would mean that body and soul were separated at an unnatural time, and this would damage the karma of both the patient and the person effecting the death.

Since violation of the principle of ahimsa brings bad karma to the killer, his life is affected, as is his future. Equally, the soul of the person killed is believed to be reincarnated with the same karma as at death; so the soul will suffer as it did before the euthanasia.

Thus Hinduism would be opposed to the practice of euthanasia.

However, some would argue that helping to end a painful life would be performing a good deed, and would fulfil moral obligations under appropriate circumstances.

Suicide, too, is contrary to Hindu morality on the grounds of ahimsa and karma. However, where a person is coming towards the end of natural life, is unable to perform normal bodily purification, and death appears imminent, it can be appropriate within Hinduism for the person to declare a purpose to fast to death, an action known as 'prayopavesa'. It is required that it be performed under community regulation, and need not rule out painkilling treatment or taking of water.[11]

Buddhism

Lama Zopa Rinpoche is a Buddhist philosopher with a deep concern for and interest in care at the end of life. He writes as follows of the Buddhist attitude to euthanasia:

> Many people see euthanasia as a compassionate act that ends the suffering of a dying person. However, performing euthanasia with a good motivation is not sufficient, because we need to help others with wisdom as well as compassion. If the person will have more peace and happiness in their next life, our action is good. On the other hand, even though our action may stop the person's present suffering, it could result in their being reborn in a realm where their suffering will be a million times worse.
>
> My concern is more for the outcome in the person's next life. If they are going to reincarnate in a hell realm, for example, it is better to keep them alive one day or even one hour longer. Since we don't have the clairvoyance to see where the person will be reborn, we have to rely upon the wisdom of fully awakened beings who have omniscience, compassion for all living beings and also the perfect power to guide us.
>
> However, in the case of someone who is going to stay in a coma for many years, rather than spending thousands of

dollars keeping them alive, it would be good to use the money to purify their negative karma which will cause them to suffer in their future lives. It would be better to spend the money to benefit many people, then dedicate the positive energy created, not only to the temporary happiness of that person, but to their liberation from all suffering and achievement of enlightenment. Giving the money to a good cause is the best thing to do. It can be done on behalf of a family member, a friend or even an enemy and can help to relieve feelings of guilt.

Whether the person is still alive or has already died, it is best to purify their negative karma. This help can come from family members and friends. Helping others with wisdom and compassion in this way makes it meaningful for us to have met, known and lived with them.[12]

Traditional Christian belief

Christianity has been opposed to euthanasia, since it holds that the gift of life and its ending are in the hands of God. Job stated the matter succinctly when he said, 'The Lord gave and the Lord has taken away; may the name of the Lord be praised!' (Job 1:21).

Roman Catholicism remains strongly opposed to euthanasia and physician-assisted suicide. Pope John Paul II described euthanasia as an example of the culture of death in Western societies, and as a manifestation of social views that have abandoned the protection of life and lent support to liberalised abortion, capital punishment and incessant warfare.[13]

Much Protestant belief would support this view, but the emphasis on individual responsibility has encouraged some Protestant theologians to claim that religious values such as compassion, mercy and love would lead to a contrary position.

Nevertheless, the Church of England's House of Bishops, and the Catholic Bishops' Conference of England and Wales, presented a united submission to the recent Select Committee of the House of Lords. They declared that it would be deeply misguided to legislate for terminally ill people to be killed or assisted in suicide. It would fundamentally undermine the basis of law and medicine, and undermine the duty of the state to care for vulnerable people.

Further, the Archbishop of Canterbury, Dr Rowan Williams, in a lecture in 2005, made a clear declaration of his position:

> The current drift towards a more accepting attitude to assisted suicide and euthanasia in some quarters gives me a great deal of concern. What begins as a compassionate desire to enable those who long for death because of protracted pain, distress or humiliation to have their wish can, with the best will in the world, help to foster an attitude that assumes resources spent on the elderly are a luxury. Investment in palliative medicine, ensuring that access to the best palliative care is universally available, continuing research not only into the causes but into the behavioural varieties of dementia and so on – how secure would these be as priorities if there were any more general acceptance of the principle that it is legitimate to initiate a process designed to end someone's life? I am certainly not ascribing to the defenders of euthanasia or assisted dying any motive but the desire to spare people unnecessary suffering. But I think we have to ask the awkward question about how this might develop in a climate of anxiety about scarce resources.[14]

4

So Why Not?

It was the end of a long evening's conference. Two of us had been talking about the issues around euthanasia to a large and interested audience. As usual there were a number of questions from people with particular experiences, some emotionally charged, some intellectually demanding. Then there were the people who wanted to talk to the speakers afterwards at a personal level. I noticed a lady in a wheelchair making her way determinedly towards me and prepared myself to counter yet another comment about the unfairness of life.

But I was due for a surprise. 'Betty' had suffered from multiple sclerosis for years, and the illness had progressed severely, but in steps, with periods of stability. Now, she explained, she was partially sighted, confined to a wheelchair for mobility, and had a permanent catheter to drain her urine as she had lost all control of her bladder. Her arms were weak and she was inclined to drop things. But, 'Don't allow euthanasia for disabled people to come in!' she said.

She told me that over the years as her condition had worsened she had had periods when the burden had seemed intolerable. 'There were three periods when I longed for the end, and, if euthanasia had been legal, I would certainly have asked for it. As it is now, however, life is so worth living that I am very glad euthanasia was not allowed.' Her illness had continued to progress and she was severely disabled, but a deep faith had dramatically affected her outlook. 'Don't let them pull the rug out from under disabled people's feet!' she urged.

Arguments against euthanasia

We can group the arguments against euthanasia under a number of headings. We shall consider whether euthanasia is necessary, what it would do to a person's dignity, and whether it would change attitudes to disabled or disadvantaged people. We need to ask who would perform the action, and what that would do to them.

Necessary?

The surgeon had made an unwelcome and unexpected discovery during the operation. What faced him was a large cancer arising from the stomach, and which had already spread to the liver – quite inoperable and unlikely to be responsive to any chemical or radiological treatment. As he closed the operation wound he said to his junior, 'The kindest thing would be for this lady not to wake up!'

In fact, the patient did wake, and was able to leave the hospital and to resume a useful life with little pain, although the length was shorter than she and her family had hoped before her illness was discovered.

Much has changed in 40 years – notably our ability to

manage symptoms arising from cancer and other incurable illnesses. Much of this advance has been due to the researches into pain and other symptoms undertaken by hospices and palliative-care teams during this same period.

We now know much more about the ways in which diseases can produce their effects, and powerful medications have been developed to relieve pain of various sorts, and to improve other symptoms. Methods of control have been widely taught, and the care of patients with incurable disease is part of the syllabus in all the medical schools in the United Kingdom – and in many other countries. At the same time, the law has been tested to ensure that doctors are able to give all appropriate medications, including the powerful painkillers related to morphine (properly called opioids), whenever they are needed to relieve pain and care for patients effectively.

A legal right to symptom relief

Miss Annie Lindsell was a person who suffered from an incurable, progressive and fatal condition called motor neurone disease. She was very anxious that her doctor might be prevented from giving her adequate doses of painkillers if and when she developed pain, supposing that at that time she was unable to request the treatment. She took her case to the courts to establish that the doctor could give all necessary relief for any pain or distress in the terminal period.

The court made it clear that it was indeed the case that all needed symptom relief could legally be given, and remarked that the case was in fact unnecessary.

Miss Lindsell died peacefully shortly after the conclusion of the case.

Indeed, the World Health Organisation has researched the effectiveness of pain relief in advanced cancer and reports that 85% of patients with pain can be relieved of their pain by the common painkillers; a further 10% can also have their pain removed by using a combination of painkillers, carefully adjusted. The remaining 5% of patients with pain ought to be able to have total relief at rest but may continue to get some pain when they are active.

The same applies to most other symptoms. We shall have more to say about pain and symptom relief. For the moment we must record that pain management and symptom control are not an adequate reason for euthanasia, but rather a cry for redoubled attention to the management of each patient. As has sometimes been said, we should not have to treat the pain by killing the patient!

We should also note that most of the research work resulting in effective pain management and symptom control has been stimulated by patients' needs. Legalised euthanasia would reduce the urgency of such studies and the drive for individual programmes of symptom relief would undoubtedly falter.

The importance of intention and the doctrine of double effect

In July 1997, Mr George Liddell was suffering from recurrent bowel cancer. He was staying with his daughter after discharge from hospital and came under the care of Dr David Moor, a General Practitioner. He had been in considerable pain and Dr Moor arranged a continuous infusion of diamorphine, a very strong painkiller, for him. The following day Dr Moor visited him at home and gave an extra injection of diamorphine, saying to the family that Mr Liddell had now only ten minutes to live. They were able to go in and say their goodbyes and shortly afterwards Mr Liddell died. Dr Moor signed a cremation form and the body was to have been cremated.

It happened that another doctor, who was medical director of the Voluntary Euthanasia Society, had told the *Sunday Times* that doctors did practise euthanasia, and that he had himself administered fatal doses to patients suffering pain and distress.

Dr Moor, a known supporter of euthanasia, was approached by a Sunday paper for his comment. He claimed he had done the same, including for a patient the previous week. Mr Liddell was identified as the patient referred to, the cremation was stopped and at a post-mortem examination the examining doctor did not find evidence of abnormality or disease that would provide adequate explanation for Mr Liddell's ultimate death, but suspected that death was due to the diamorphine injected.

The prosecuting barrister stated that the prosecution case was that Dr Moor deliberately ended the life of George Liddell by administering a fatal dose of diamorphine. His primary intention had been to end life. The trial was not about the merits and demerits of euthanasia, or mercy-killing, but of a doctor deliberately ending the life of a patient in his care. In his defence, Dr Moor said he did not deliberately kill Mr Liddell, but gave the diamorphine to relieve his pain knowing that he was likely to die, but not knowing for sure that he would die as a consequence. Despite his previous statements to the press and on television he now said that he had never set out to kill anyone, though he had certainly set out to ease discomfort and distress and to give patients a pain-free death.

Eventually, the jury cleared Dr Moor on the grounds that his intention had been to relieve pain rather than to kill his patient. After the case the Detective Superintendent who headed the enquiry said: 'To a police officer and the criminal justice system, the terms "mercy-killing" and "euthanasia" are meaningless. If you shorten someone's life by minutes, that's murder, and by law we had to approach our investigation from this viewpoint.'

One useful outcome of the acquittal was to underline that a painkiller can rightly be given to relieve pain, even if that might in the end shorten the sufferer's life. This is called the doctrine of double effect.

Double effect

We need to think about whether the sort of doses of painkillers we are using might themselves shorten the life of our patients. As the case of Mr Liddell and Dr Moor shows, it is accepted that the risk of possibly shortening a person's life should not stop us giving adequate pain relief. The purpose of the medication is to relieve pain, not to terminate life. If a possible side effect might be that life is shortened, this is acceptable ethically and legally. The principle is that medications may have two effects: the intended useful one; and also a foreseen possibility, but not a necessary consequence, of harm. This is the so-called doctrine of double effect.

But common experience of medical staff caring for people with advanced cancer is that effective doses of pain-relieving medicines do not shorten life. I remember someone being brought to the hospice desperately ill with very advanced cancer. We will call her Jenny. She had fought against leaving home until pain, diarrhoea and vomiting had made coping impossible. After examining her I had to tell her that I could not cure her but was sure we could relieve her pain and sickness. I said, 'I'm afraid there is not much time left, perhaps three or four days, but we'll make it as good as possible.'

'I understand that,' said Jenny. 'My doctor told me there were only two or three days left, but if you can take this pain away it will be wonderful.'

After an injection Jenny slept soundly. A steady supply of medication kept her comfortable. The following morning, when I went to see her, she said that the pain had gone ten minutes after the injection, the nausea had disappeared in two hours and she had had a good night and a cup of tea this morning. 'When will breakfast be coming?' she asked!

Two days later she was walking with the support of two nurses and a week later she was telling her story to a visiting reporter. Jenny needed to be reminded that she was not cured! She did die very peacefully in her sleep six weeks after our considered opinion that she had only a few days left.

Errors of diagnosis and prognosis

And that, too, is an issue with euthanasia. Doctors do sometimes get the diagnosis wrong, as well as the timing of the outlook (known as the prognosis). Sometimes it is difficult to make an accurate diagnosis when, for example, the patient is too poorly to undergo particular investigations – or refuses to have them performed. In other cases the tests do not give a definite answer. And in other cases what seemed a very clear diagnosis proves erroneous.

I knew of a lady who was admitted to a hospice after an operation for a kidney cancer. Tests had shown evidence of secondary growths in spine and liver, and the news was broken to her and her family that time would now be short. However, months later she was definitely better and it became evident that the 'bone secondaries' were in fact wear-and-tear changes and the 'liver secondaries' were inoffensive cysts. The removal of the kidney had been a curative procedure. In this case, the 'good news' that the patient was not suffering from cancer at all proved very difficult for patient and family to accept, as all had got used to living with her very short outlook!

We have also seen occasions – rarely, it must be admitted – when proven cancer has been completely and miraculously cured. Such a person was Audrey, who came to the hospice after an operation to remove a large part of her liver and gall bladder for a cancer. Audrey was told that the operation could not be curative and she had a very stormy recovery period in hospital. She came to the hospice deeply jaundiced and both she and we thought she would die. She had recently made a Christian commitment and much prayer was said for her. A month later the jaundice was less, and she told me that she was suddenly aware that God was preserving her life for a purpose. From then on there was a steady recovery and she returned home some months later – to nurse her sister who had also developed a cancer, and to care for the family. We continue to be in contact 15 years later.

Such events, where a diagnosis or prognosis proved dramatically wrong, should make us extremely cautious about termination of life on the grounds of symptoms from an illness presumed to be incurable.

Dignity?

'I just want her to die with dignity.' We not infrequently hear such comments, and then the relative sometimes goes on to say, 'If she was a dog you'd have her put down.' I remember an elderly lady in a nursing home saying to me, 'But I'm not a dog and I'm grateful for people who provide human support and care.'

Dignity has to do with worth. We demean people if we think all they are worth is a procured death. People are worth human care, just by virtue of who they are, not because they can do something or earn a living. At this point we do well to remember the horror of the extermination camps under the Nazis in the Second World War.

This affront to human dignity started with the decision to permit euthanasia in Nazi Germany before the war. From 1922 there had been agitation for legalisation of euthanasia. In that year a proposal to legalise it was put to the German parliament, but was rejected. In the mid-1930s a baby was born blind and deformed. The baby's condition was widely publicised and, in response to a campaign, Hitler authorised his doctor to give a lethal injection to the baby. This became a precedent for killing all newborn babies who were in any way defective. This was extended to older children, then to children up to the age of 16. Respect for parents' wishes was dropped.

Ordinary people made no objection to a practice which was so easily justified as kindness. From a means of releasing from suffering it progressed easily to become a means of 'cleansing' a race from disabled and disadvantaged members, and then to people who were regarded as an alien race. The result was six million people exterminated in the holocaust. What a slippery slope! We have to continue to guard against any practice which demeans the value of another human being, and that includes the concept that someone's life is not worth living.

We started the chapter with Betty, who was, by any measure, greatly disabled. She feared that the introduction of euthanasia, even with the best motives, would lead to its application to people who were disabled. At times of physical or psychological distress, such people might well request euthanasia as a way out – as she claimed she would have done. Frail, elderly and disabled people do come to believe that their lives are not worth living. If we were to agree to a request for euthanasia, that would only reinforce their belief that they were worth nothing to anyone.

Once it was an accepted practice, people who were disabled or chronically ill might be encouraged to accept euthanasia. They might feel themselves to be a drain on their family or on society, and would come to request euthanasia as a sacrifice they could make for their relatives or for society. After all, other people thought that their lives were not worth living. In this way, subtle pressure would be experienced by such people, leading to requests for euthanasia. And if this became the case for disabled people, what about those who were regarded as a drain on the economy; and the racially different; and. . .? It is easy to think that this would not happen in our country, but it was in our country at a conference on euthanasia that I heard just such arguments being used.

Kind?

Some years ago the chairman of a national society seeking to promote euthanasia himself developed cancer. He was treated actively but the cancer could not be eradicated. He received good medical care for his symptoms. However, he had been vigorous in his promotion of the value of euthanasia and now he could not assure himself that his doctors were not seeking to put his previous views into action. He became so anxious that perhaps his carers might give him medication for euthanasia that he sought out the local hospice doctor and asked him to take over his care because he knew that this doctor, at least, would not practise euthanasia!

Isn't it interesting that the possibility of euthanasia can introduce a burden of guilt and fear for patients, their families and for professional carers?

Some frail, elderly and disabled people would feel that they ought to have requested euthanasia for the sake of the family or society. One can imagine a sense of guilt many of them might feel. There would certainly be a fear – as is reported to be the case among some elderly folk in the Netherlands where euthanasia is legalised – that they might well be future candidates.

For families of people who had undergone euthanasia, there would be a self-questioning and a prolonged sense of guilt. In the normal grieving process that follows any death or loss, one of the emotions experienced is commonly a sense of guilt. 'If only I'd done such and such. . . or not done so and so. . . then perhaps he would not have died.' This occurs even when there is no reason for self-reproach; how much more would this be true if the relatives had had a part in encouraging or agreeing to a request for euthanasia!

During occasional discussions with people who have claimed that they had been involved in euthanasia decisions, I have sensed a self-justification which appears to spring from just such a feeling of suppressed guilt.

Whose autonomy?

But is it only patients and relatives who are involved? How would professionals feel about being asked to perform euthanasia? What about their autonomy? Would they carry a sense of guilt?

Does it have to be doctors who perform the euthanasia? We may notice here that in Oregon, where assisted suicide is legal, doctors prescribe the necessary drugs but the person administers them to him or herself. In Switzerland the act can be performed by anyone, and does not need a doctor. In the United Kingdom recently the Royal College of General Practitioners reversed a decision to take a neutral stand on the issue of whether euthanasia should be legalised; they would oppose it and would prefer that doctors were not involved!

Doctors and nurses are trained to care for and to use their skills in curing and supporting ill people. Acting deliberately to terminate life would seriously compromise their practice and would change the doctor–patient relationship. In hospice I sometimes have to reassure people who have been admitted and who are afraid that their lives will be shortened. It is always good to be able to tell them unequivocally that people's lives are not shortened in hospice. I would find it much more difficult if hospice were a place for mercy-killing, even occasionally. Would they be reassured if we had to say, 'No, we don't usually kill people here'?

Undermining respect for life

In 1994 a Select Committee of the House of Lords reported on medical ethics and the law relating to issues at the end of life. In recommending that there should be no change in the law to permit euthanasia, they pointed out that prohibition of intentional killing was the cornerstone of law and of social relationships. It protected each one of us impartially, they said, embodying the belief that all are equal in the eyes of the law, even if some are frailer than others and some are disabled in one respect or another.

Conclusion

We have seen that there are a number of good reasons to which we can point against the practice of euthanasia. A group of sixth-form young people was debating the issue of the legalisation of euthanasia. Their conclusion after carefully and dispassionately weighing the evidence was that euthanasia was emotionally attractive but socially disastrous. That is the argument of this chapter.

5

Hard Cases

There is another serious implication of legalising voluntary euthanasia. We have already touched on the matter of involuntary and non-voluntary euthanasia when we looked at definitions at the beginning of Chapter 2. It now becomes relevant to ask whether any legalisation of euthanasia could or should be restricted to people who request it. The issue is relevant because of recent legal decisions in the United States and the United Kingdom; because of current questions being faced and answered in the Netherlands, Belgium and Switzerland; and because of issues being debated in the United Kingdom.

A few years ago the *British Medical Journal* published a disturbing leading article. In effect the authors asked what the importance of 'voluntariness' was if it was a moral good to legalise the termination of life of people for whom life was no longer worth living and for whom death was preferable to life. If we agreed that severe physical disability (even in the absence of pain) would be a reason to respond to a request for euthanasia, why should severely disabled people who cannot request euthanasia be denied it? If we agreed that despair in terminally ill people with a fatal illness was a ground for euthanasia, why should despairing people without a fatal illness be denied it? If life that could never be worthwhile because of advanced illness was a ground for euthanasia when requested, why should it be denied to people who could never recover from persisting unconsciousness or vegetative state? In other words, can we properly say that some lives are simply not worth living, and because of that should be terminated?

But before we look at that last question, let us meet four groups of people. We will need to meet 'Auntie Maud' (of Chapter 2) and her brother 'Uncle Jack'; Terri Schiavo and Tony Bland in a persistent vegetative state; some people who have been deeply depressed for years; and a very badly deformed newly born infant. I'm sorry, but they each raise vital questions! This chapter is entitled 'Hard Cases', and you are entitled to skip it if you wish – or hasten to the conclusions! And we do indeed remember the old saying that hard cases make bad law. But that is precisely why we need to discuss the issues these people raise before they come upon us, unsuspected.

We will remember that some of these are represented among the more than a thousand people provided with euthanasia in 1989 in the Netherlands without requesting it. And a similar thousand or more people each year since, as the surveys of 1995 and 2001 showed. The legalisation of voluntary euthanasia seems to have made no difference to the number of these – still illegal – involuntary cases. But this is not solely a Dutch issue: some of the people we shall meet are – or were – alive in England.

Advanced senile dementia

Our first candidate is 'Auntie Maud', who is a fictitious character representing many elderly folk suffering from senile dementia. You will remember that she has been in a nursing home for years, looking lost and unable to recognise her visitors. People ask questions about local equivalents of Auntie Maud whenever we speak about euthanasia. Sadly, with lengthening life expectancy in the United Kingdom and elsewhere in the Western world, there comes a rising population of elderly (and not-so-elderly) people with senile and pre-senile dementia.

In 2005 just such a patient at an earlier stage in his illness requested physician assistance to commit suicide in the Netherlands. His was the first such case to be reported to the Netherlands' assessment committee after the death. The patient was 65 and had suffered from Alzheimer's disease for three years. Since his diagnosis he had said he did not wish to survive the full course of the disease and during his final year had asked persistently for help with suicide. His doctor believed he was suffering unbearably because he was unable to function independently and faced a prospect of increasing dementia. A second opinion was sought, but this doctor, who had been trained to take such decisions, did not recognise in him unbearable suffering and therefore did not support the request for euthanasia. However, he was referred to other doctors, who concluded there was such suffering and that the patient remained competent at that point in time. He was therefore assisted to commit suicide. Physician-assisted suicide is, of course, voluntary; but it illustrates the issue we are addressing.

Initially, such sufferers experience increasing forgetfulness for recent events and conversations. Gradually the timescale of the memory loss increases, disorientation occurs as to where he or she is and forgetfulness of who other people are. The person may undergo a significant change of personality, becoming irritable, irrational and increasingly uninhibited. Over months or years it may become difficult to cope with Auntie Maud at home, and she may need to go into a nursing home where she (or her brother, Uncle Jack) will need constant observation, supervision and care, perhaps for some years. There the disorientation, restlessness and loss of personal dignity continue to worsen.

And the family ask, 'Could they not be put out of their misery?'

As we showed, this would not be voluntary euthanasia because Auntie Maud and Uncle Jack have not requested it – and did not, even in their lucid moments. Is that because they would never have asked for termination of their life, or simply because they would not have understood or thought of the possibility? But would they have wished it? And does it matter what they would have wished, since now they are so mentally and, perhaps, physically disabled?

We are reminded of some such 'Auntie Mauds' and 'Uncle Jacks' who seem totally unaware of where they are and who their visitors are. Yet if those visitors will start a hymn tune, Auntie Maud or Uncle Jack will join in with all the words and obviously find meaning and pleasure in the sharing. Indeed, for many such, even when they have no church connection, memory of songs and tunes from earlier days remains an important link with their former selves, and says to us that 'in there somewhere' they are still Maud or Jack, and deserve the dignity and care we can offer.

Persistent vegetative state

Some of the most publicised cases in recent years have been people in what is known as a persistent vegetative state. These are people who have suffered a severe head injury or brain damage due to lack of oxygen to the brain – often because of a heart attack or stroke – and who have failed to regain consciousness. In most people with these injuries attempts at resuscitation either fail and are followed by the patient's death, or succeed in improving the situation so that recovery of consciousness occurs within a matter of hours or days.

Once the person is out of immediate danger, though still in coma or unconsciousness, medical care concentrates on preventing infections and maintaining the patient's physical state. Such people need to be fed through a tube if they remain unable to feed themselves. Evacuation of bowels and bladder is managed or assisted by the carers. Limbs are put through a full range of movements daily to prevent joints seizing up. Attendants, carers and family if possible try to stimulate the 'sleeping brain' with music, speech and questions.

In the vast majority of cases of coma, where death does not occur within days, there is recovery from the unconsciousness within two to four weeks. The longer the coma persists the poorer is the outlook. In a very small number of patients a limited recovery occurs, in that these people are able to breathe independently and to move their limbs.

They may appear reasonably normal, opening their eyes, grimacing, even crying or laughing. But, tragically, they are unable to respond to people or events around them. Movements are not purposeful and it is evident that they have lost the function of the thinking parts of the brain – the cerebral hemispheres – in part or in whole. If this state continues, the condition is described as a vegetative state, which, by definition, becomes a persistent vegetative state (PVS) after a year from the incident.

The majority of such patients do die with an infection (usually of chest, bladder or kidneys); but others linger and may make a partial recovery, even some years later. In rare cases that recovery may be virtually to completely normal independent life, even after four years in PVS, as I have witnessed. A recent patient in the United States made a remarkable recovery, according to a television report, after 18 years – although he had permanently lost a considerable part of the thinking and learning area of his brain. He was unable to appreciate that 18 years had elapsed or fully to relate to people. Specialists tell us that there is a wide spectrum of severity of condition in patients with PVS, such that for some recovery may be possible while for others the outlook is extremely poor.

Several patients in PVS have become unwittingly embroiled in legal cases about cessation of tube feeding and whether this constitutes involuntary euthanasia. One of these was Tony Bland in Sheffield, who was in PVS from 1989 till his death after removal of the feeding tube in 1993. We recount his story in Chapter 8. Another prolonged and tragic case was that of Terri Schiavo, who illustrates the complexity of decision-making for such people.

Terri Schiavo – persistent vegetative state and family conflict

In 1990 in the USA 26-year-old Terri Schiavo suffered a heart attack and her heart stopped beating. She was resuscitated but remained in a persistent vegetative state for the next 15 years. She was married to Michael and was supported by him, by her parents, Bobby Schindler and his wife, and by her siblings, but there was no recovery. She remained unable to swallow or to communicate, although she smiled, cried and even (according to her parents) uttered a few simple words. She was tube-fed throughout these 15 years, and for much of the time was nursed in a hospice in Florida. In 1998 Terri's husband went to court to ask for the feeding tube to be removed on the grounds of absence of any hope of recovery. Terri's parents opposed the case as they were convinced Terri could yet recover. From 1998 until March 2005 legal actions continued. Terri had left no instructions about how she would wish to be treated in such a situation, but her mother always claimed she would not wish to die.

The Florida courts respected Michael Schiavo's request that Terri be allowed to die with dignity following removal of the feeding tube. Five years after the original court hearing, in response to the parents' appeal, the Florida Lower House passed 'Terri's Law'. This allowed the Florida Governor to order doctors to feed Mrs Schiavo. A year later the Florida Supreme Court reversed that law, and six months later the Florida court allowed doctors to remove the tube. Terri died twelve days after the tube's removal despite appeals which went up to the

United States Supreme Court, and involved the support of the State Governor and his brother, Mr George Bush, President of the United States, who was against the removal of the feeding tube.

Sadly, there was dissension between parents and husband even during Terri's dying period. Newspapers report that at the end she was being cradled by her husband, and that her brother was present in the room, but her father had apparently been ordered out.

At post-mortem examination the pathologist reported that Mrs Schiavo's brain had suffered very severe damage (it seems as a result of the original oxygen-starvation) and supported the diagnosis of irreversible persistent vegetative state.

Are these people, whose injury or illness resulted in the severest form of persistent vegetative state, persons suffering a prolonged dying from which they should be released and for whom the use of advanced and costly resources is futile? Or are they severely disabled people whose life should be protected at all costs? Or can some sort of balance be struck?

Unremitting depression and non-fatal illnesses

Within two years of the Dutch decision to legalise euthanasia there was a request from a lady who was depressed and stated that, for her, life was no longer worth living. She was a widow who had had two sons. One had died young and the other, learning of his brother's death, had committed suicide. Mother had become severely depressed and said she had nothing to live for. She did not respond to anti-depressant medication and requested euthanasia. The request was granted.

We noted in Chapter 3 that Dutch law does not specify that the applicant for euthanasia has to be suffering from a fatal illness, but that the suffering has to be unbearable and hopeless and that there must be a persistent and well-considered request. Hence this request from the severely depressed widow fell within the definition. Would that become appropriate in the United Kingdom?

Here was voluntary euthanasia, certainly. But is this evidence of expanding of the indications for euthanasia beyond what was initially envisaged when the law was introduced in the Netherlands? How unbearable does 'unbearable suffering' have to be? And where does hopelessness receive its limits?

We are exploring in this chapter the difficulty of setting boundaries once the principle has been accepted that terminating people's lives is acceptable under certain conditions. How can one set ethically acceptable limits? We saw at the beginning of the chapter that some medical ethicists are asking how widely the limits can be drawn. Limits of any sort disqualify some who would wish to be included.

When the Abortion Act was passed it was in order to bring within the law a current practice, to control it, and allow it to be safe and well regulated. Who thought that within 35 years there would have been over five million legal abortions performed in the United Kingdom? Who envisaged all the reasons for abortion that are now accepted?

Which brings us to our fourth group of hard cases.

Neonatal euthanasia

Euthanasia for newborn babies cannot be voluntary except in the way that abortion seeks only the wishes of the parents. Is it sufficient that the parents request it, or agree to the doctor's recommendation?

In July 2005 the *British Medical Journal* reported that eminently respectable Dutch paediatricians (children's doctors) had voted unanimously to adopt a set of proposals to cover the mercy-killing of newborn babies who were incurably sick and suffering severely. These proposals were drawn up by the paediatricians at the Groningen University Hospital and are known as the Groningen protocol.

The clinical director explained his very great dilemma. In a very few cases each year – perhaps 15 out of 200,000 live births in a year in Holland – the infant was found to be suffering from a severe malformation or congenital illness which was incurable, which would very significantly affect the child's development, and which was causing or would cause severe suffering.

He instanced an infant with an exceedingly rare inherited skin disease which resulted in blistering on contact, exposing the infant to infection and causing pain whenever dressings on the exposed area were changed. Other examples would be the worst varieties of spina bifida (where the skin and bony covering of the spinal cord are deficient in the lower back) with associated brain damage; or the most extreme effects of oxygen-starvation of the brain at birth, resulting in damage to brain, lungs and heart and perhaps continual convulsions.

The protocols would require:

- a clear diagnosis and prognosis (assessment of future outlook)
- that the newborn must be suffering hopelessly and unbearably with no prospect for future treatment
- that both parents must give their informed consent
- that the decision must be confirmed by a second independent doctor
- that the death and treatment must be reported to the local coroner.

It was envisaged that the protocol would legitimise what was currently being practised in a covert way and would encourage practitioners to report their actions to a national committee. The paediatricians asked the Dutch political authorities to legislate appropriately.

We may ask what happens in the United Kingdom. British paediatricians point to the advance of the principles of palliative care; the widespread acceptance of the doctrine of double effect for pain and symptom relief; and, in a similar way to the Netherlands, the very high standard of paediatric medical and surgical care available. Professor John Wyatt, in his book *Matters of Life and Death*,[1] gives a careful and relevant review of the issues from the point of view of a senior Christian paediatrician.

Conclusions

The presence of these four groups of hard cases helps us to see some of the areas where boundaries are difficult to define. In all these areas people will claim they are being discriminated against if their requests are not agreed.

At the beginning of the chapter we asked what was so special about 'voluntariness'. If some people's lives are not worth living and they request euthanasia under strictly regulated circumstances, then legalised euthanasia would require it to be done. But suppose those same circumstances exist and the person is unable (because of dementia, unconsciousness or infancy, for example) to make a request. Their carers believe their life is not worth living. Then should they be denied euthanasia?

But are we not here drifting down the slippery slope experienced in Germany in the 1930s, and is not the end of that slope euthanasia for anybody whose life someone else in authority feels is pointless? Somewhere a line has to be drawn, and where better than at the beginning of the slope?

6

Is There a Biblical Viewpoint?

We are 'worth' a great deal to God!

> Are not two sparrows sold for a penny? Yet not one of them
> will fall to the ground apart from the will of your Father. And
> even the very hairs of your head are all numbered. So don't be
> afraid; you are worth more than many sparrows. (Jesus in
> Matthew 10:29–31)

In this chapter we must try to unwrap what that statement
means in relation to our subject.

Jesus' teaching and example

You won't find the word 'euthanasia' in the Bible. There is,
however, one specific command that is relevant. The sixth
of the Ten Commandments reads, 'You shall not murder'
(Exodus 20:13). Jesus quoted this commandment specifically in his Sermon on the Mount as the first of the commandments he wished to amplify in his teaching.

Listen to him as he teaches his disciples on the moun-
tainside about his relationship to the Law given through

Moses centuries earlier: teaching recorded for us by Matthew in chapter 5 of his Gospel. The teaching opens with the Beatitudes – those sayings of blessedness, happiness, even congratulations, upon people who are upholding God's standards of love and grace. Then, after calling his followers to be salt and light in the community, he says:

> Do not think that I have come to abolish the Law or the Prophets; I have not come to abolish them but to fulfil them. I tell you the truth, until heaven and earth disappear, not the smallest letter, not the least stroke of a pen, will by any means disappear from the Law until everything is accomplished. (Matthew 5:17–18)

For Jesus' hearers, the Law was the Jewish system of rules based upon the Ten Commandments. Jesus upholds their authority. He insists, before commenting on individual commandments, that he is in no way abrogating the Law. He will actually extend its impact into word and thought. He goes on:

> Anyone who breaks one of the least of these commandments and teaches others to do the same will be called least in the kingdom of heaven, but whoever practises and teaches these commands will be called great in the kingdom of heaven. For I tell you that unless your righteousness surpasses that of the Pharisees and the teachers of the law, you will certainly not enter the kingdom of heaven. (Matthew 5:19–20)

Then, lest anyone should question which part of the Law he particularly has in mind, he goes on to take a number of examples. And the first is the sixth commandment:

> You have heard that it was said to the people long ago, 'Do not murder, and anyone who murders will be subject to

judgment.' But I tell you that anyone who is angry with his brother will be subject to judgment. Again, anyone who says to his brother, 'Raca' [Stupid idiot] is answerable to the Sanhedrin. But anyone who says 'You fool!' will be in danger of the fire of hell. Therefore, if you . . . remember that your brother has something against you . . . first, go and be reconciled to your brother . . . (vv. 21–24)

He goes on to amplify the seventh, ninth and tenth commandments, so he is not being selective! He is, however, underlining for us that the Ten Commandments are still God's will for his people – and that includes the sixth commandment.

We must set the teaching of Jesus in the context of who he is, and what his nature tells us about God's attitude to people in their suffering – the subject of our book.

God's value on human life

The Bible tells us that in Jesus, God, the creator and sustainer of life, took on himself human form. 'In the beginning was the Word, and the Word was with God, and the Word was God . . . The Word became flesh and made his dwelling among us.' And John, the disciple, adds his own testimony, 'We have seen his glory, the glory of the One and Only, who came from the Father, full of grace and truth' (John 1:1,14). So God demonstrates not only his love for mankind, but also his acceptance of the fleshly body, with all its attendant weaknesses.

We remember that this Jesus was not born to live in a palace – as would befit a human prince, let alone God-made-man – but was born in a stable because there was no room available in the bed-and-breakfast accommodation of the day. He was shortly to become an infant refugee, displaced with his human parents to neighbouring Egypt. Later, grown up and educated in a backwater of Galilee, where he had plied the trade of a carpenter until he started his itinerant ministry, he would say, 'Foxes have holes and birds of the air have nests, but the Son of Man [his favourite term for himself] has nowhere to lay his head' (Matthew 8:20).

In all of this he was identifying himself with mankind in all its weakness.

God's desire for our wholeness and healing

We notice, because the people of his day noticed, Jesus' care and compassion for people who were sick and suffering. The first two years of Jesus' teaching and preaching are full of stories of his healing people in response to their appeals to him.

I particularly love the first chapter of Mark's Gospel where he records what we might call 'A Day in the Life of a Preacher'! During the morning synagogue worship Jesus' teaching is interrupted by a deranged man's shriek. Jesus sets him free from his spirit-possession. He then heals Peter's mother-in-law's fever so completely that she gets up to prepare lunch! Word of Jesus' presence and his healing spreads rapidly, and in the evening people bring a crowd of sick folk to be healed – and Jesus heals many and provides wonderful symptom control as well!

Early next morning Jesus goes out of town to find a quiet place to pray and gain strength for the new day's walking and teaching – and healing. Is it on this morning that he and the disciples are met by the man with leprosy (Mark 1:40)? 'If you want to, you can make me clean' ('like you did for many with other afflictions yesterday', he might have added). So Jesus, filled with compassion, reaches out his hand and touches the man. Oh, the grace of that action! It is the first time the man has been touched by any non-leper since his disease has been diagnosed. And Jesus has no gloves! Then, after touching him, Jesus says (my interpretation), 'Of course I want to! Be clean!' 'Immediately the leprosy left him and he was healed,' says Mark.

Not only does Jesus do these loving healings; he also raises the dead, on at least three occasions (Jairus's daughter, the widow of Nain's son and Lazarus). Why only three? Were there more but only three are recorded? Perhaps. But we must also remember that each of these had to die again – there is no one in Israel who is 2,000 years old! So each, and their families, had to go through the dying and grieving again. Perhaps it is because it would not have been kind to them or their families that Jesus did not raise more people from the dead.

We need to note also that Jesus did not heal everybody he saw. In Acts 3 we are told about the healing through Peter and John of the cripple who had been laid daily at the gate of the temple. He had been crippled from birth and was now over 40 years old. Jesus must have seen him, but perhaps he had never asked for help. There were also others at the pool of Bethesda when Jesus healed another crippled man (John 5).

We must add that Jesus promises to be with his people till 'the end of the age', and to respond to their prayers in their need. This Jesus, who knows our suffering from the human side, and is able to do something about it, is with us in our times of need, and understands when we feel we cannot stand any more. He's been there! And so must we, as Christian people, be there when people are crying out in their need that they cannot go on.

And this understanding, sympathy and healing is not all!

God's dignifying of human suffering and death

Worse than being born in a manger, or living as a refugee or a homeless preacher, Jesus accepts the pain and degradation of mockery and scourging, the bleeding and misery of torture, and finally the criminal's death of crucifixion. If ever there was death without dignity, this was it!

He refuses analgesia (pain-relief medication) (Matthew 27:34) until the very end – but then accepts it and so makes it acceptable for his followers to do so (Matthew 27:48 and John 19:30). He dies our death, and, like us, is buried, according to the testimony of all four evangelists and Paul (1 Corinthians 15:3–4). He does not call on angels, or even his Father, for relief or release; although he was tempted in his human weakness to do so in the Garden of Gethsemane (Mark 14:35–37 and parallels).

Paul says (perhaps quoting a very early Christian hymn):

Christ Jesus
... being in very nature God,
did not consider equality with God something to be grasped,
   but made himself nothing,
taking the very nature of a servant,
being made in human likeness.
And being found in appearance as a man,
he humbled himself and became obedient unto death – even
   death on a cross! (Philippians 2:5–8)

In this way, Jesus, Son of God, accepts our body, our life and our death.

He, too, could have avoided the suffering which he fore-saw so clearly in Gethsemane. But, despite the human desire to do so, he said in effect that euthanasia (literally, 'a good dying') was not for him: 'Not my will, but yours be done,' he said (Luke 22:42). In going through the cruellest of sufferings, Jesus both gave us the example and can give us the strength to overcome in our dying.

God's love for humanity

Why should God humble himself in Jesus, in the way Paul speaks about?

John, perhaps quoting Jesus himself, says that it is because 'God so loved the world that he gave his one and only Son, that whoever believes in him should not perish but have eternal life' (John 3:16). I am amazed – and so thankful – that God should set so high a value on human beings that he sent his own Son to live our life in our flesh and experience our worst privations.

But Jesus says it was for more than that that he came! Mark records him saying, 'The Son of Man did not come to be served, but to serve, and to give his life as a ransom for many' (Mark 10:45). Matthew, Mark and Luke – and Paul, in one of his letters – record that at the Last Supper Jesus gave the cup to his disciples, saying, 'This is my blood of the covenant, which is poured out for many' (Mark 14:24 and parallels). As we speak of the life and death of the Lord Jesus we cannot forget that he died in our place, to bring us forgiveness, peace with God and eternal life as we believe in him. In his great chapter about death and resurrection, Paul comes to the climax: 'Death has been swallowed up in victory. Where, O death, is your victory? Where, O death, is your sting?' (1 Corinthians 15:54–55).

The love of God for fallen and hopeless mankind was so great that he dignified human life, and human suffering and dying, with his own self.

It appears that this was the only way for God to save mankind from the consequences of sin: if there had been a cheaper way for God to take, would he not have done so? But in what he did, he dignified human weakness and need, and set the highest value on human life.

Our thinking about the life and death of Jesus leads us to a number of conclusions:

1. He had compassion on people who were sick and felt at the end of their tether. We believe he still cares, and so should we as his followers.
2. He did not seek a quick way out of suffering, or an easy way of dying, and he does not indicate that we may.
3. He gives no permission to take anyone's life for any reason, but endorses and strengthens the old command not to murder.
4. He evidently believed that God his Father had a perfect will about his dying, and he was willing to trust himself to that will.

We started this chapter by quoting Jesus' teaching in the Sermon on the Mount about our worth in God's sight. This leads us on to ask whether the Bible has anything more to say about the standing and worth of human life. And for this we must look back to the account of creation.

Respect for life, or sanctity of human life?

In much of this book we talk about respect for human life. This terminology is acceptable to most religious and non-religious people. It allows us to discuss matters of life and death without having to argue about creation and a specific Bible viewpoint that may not be accepted by others. A perfectly reasonable argument can be made for or against euthanasia on the grounds of respect for life. However, we may want to ask whether for the Christian there is not a deeper argument. So here goes!

Creation

In Genesis 1 the Bible speaks of three great acts of creation. In verse 1 we read, 'God created the heavens and the earth.' In verse 21, it says, 'God created the great creatures . . . and every living and moving thing with which the water teems.' And in verse 27 we read, 'God created man . . .' Everywhere else the record is that 'God made . . .'.

This is not the place to enter into discussion about creation, guided evolution, days or periods, and such matters! However, the record is quite clear that something very specific and different happened with the creation of matter (v. 1), of life (v. 21) and of man (v. 27). It is with the last that we are concerned here.

There are three accounts of the creation of man – in Genesis 1:26–30, 2:7 and 5:1–2. The first of these gives us:

- God's intention (v. 26)
- God's action (v. 27)
- God's commission (vv. 28–30).

And the third account repeats these in briefer form (Genesis 5:1–2).

> Then God said, 'Let us make man in our image, in our likeness, and let them rule over the fish of the sea and the birds of the air, over the livestock, over all the earth, and over all the creatures that move along the ground.'

> > So God created man
> > in his own image,
> > in the image of God
> > he created him;
> > male and female
> > he created them.

> God blessed them and said to them, 'Be fruitful and increase in number; fill the earth and subdue it. Rule over the fish of the sea and the birds of the air and over every living creature that moves on the ground.' (Genesis 1:26–29)

Three times we read that man is made – created – in God's image and in God's likeness. Three times we read the statement that God created man, and created them male and female – i.e. 'man' is mankind. And then we read that man(kind) is given a specific set of tasks: to be fruitful; to increase in numbers; and to be stewards over the rest of God's earthly creation.

In the second of the Genesis earth-making stories (Genesis 2:5–25) we are told of the specific formation of the first man, Adam. He is formed from what already exists ('the dust of the ground'), and 'the breath of life' is breathed into his nostrils by the Lord God and man becomes 'a living being'. He is then given tasks in an idyllic placement (the

Garden of Eden); namely to work in it and to take care of it (v. 15), and to 'name' the creatures of God's making. Finally, the Lord God makes man a helper suitable for him: a woman, Eve, who becomes his wife.

For our discussion it is important to note that the second story underlines the truth in the first: that man is a different order of creation from the rest of God's creation. In both, man carries a very specific divine imprint – the image of God, the likeness of God or the breath of life inbreathed by God.

Of course, the next chapter is to tell of the Fall of man from his position of grace, and his being turned out of the Garden of Eden. Adam and Eve are given a much harder inheritance of labour and pain in the fulfilment of their (same) tasks of being fruitful, increasing in numbers and being stewards to take care of God's wider creation (Genesis 3:16–19).

> When God created man, he made him in the likeness of God. He created them male and female and blessed them. And when they were created he called them 'man'. When Adam had lived 130 years, he had a son in his own likeness, in his own image; and he named him Seth . . . (Genesis 5:1–3)

We note that the third account (Genesis 5:1–2), re-emphasises the truth that God created man, created him in the image of God, created them male and female, and blessed them. That account continues by introducing the family line from Adam. But whereas man was created in the likeness of God, his son Seth is in his own likeness, after his own image (v. 3).

Nevertheless, it appears clear from these accounts that mankind carries the divine imprint, marred by the Fall, but nevertheless God's. If that is so, then we are right to speak of the sanctity of life.

Covenants

After the account of the Fall of man and its results, comes the account of the fulfilling of the commission to be fruitful and fill the earth. Genesis 5 has the account of the family tree from Adam, noting also the labour and painful toil included in the results of sin. Immediately after this we read of the spreading of mankind on the earth and the spreading of man's sinfulness, so much so that 'the Lord was grieved that he had made man on the earth, and his heart was filled with pain' (Genesis 6:6). There follows the account of the flood and of the saving in the ark of the family of Noah, the one righteous person, and the animal creation with him.

At the end of the story of the flood we find the first of God's covenants with man. In Genesis 9 God declares a covenant of peace between man and God, dependent on man's obedience. And the one major condition of this first covenant of God with man is the prohibition of the killing of man because 'in the image of God has God made man' (vv. 5–6):

> For your lifeblood I will surely demand an accounting. I will demand an accounting from every animal. And from each man, too, I will demand an accounting for the life of his fellow man.

> Whoever sheds the blood of man,
>   by man shall his blood be shed;
> for in the image of God
>   has God made man.

As for you, be fruitful and increase in number; multiply on the earth and increase upon it. (Genesis 9:5–7)

Later in Genesis we have God's covenants with Abraham. Exodus brings us to the great covenant at Sinai with the Ten Commandments inscribed by the hand of God on tablets of stone for his people, Israel. We have already considered the sixth commandment – 'You shall not murder' – and the way Jesus underlined and developed it.

The covenants or agreements of God with man are paralleled by other covenants of the ancient world. Like these divine covenants they are binding agreements which can be between a person and his equal or may be between a ruler and his people. They have a standard form, including a statement of the parties to the agreement, the promised benefits from the one to the other, and the terms or conditions under which the promises will be upheld, and warnings against breaking the terms of the covenant.

So it is with each of these covenant agreements between God and mankind or with his people Israel. We have the named parties to the agreement. We have a list of the benefits that God will give to his people. We are told the conditions under which the covenant will be operative and we are warned of the consequences of disobedience. And in at least three of these covenants, from the earliest (to Adam and to Noah) to the latest (the Ten Commandments), we find the command not to kill people.

Commands

These commands are not the whim of God for controlling rebellious people, but declarations of his loving concern for the people's best interests. So although the covenants from Abraham onwards are given to one nation, they make clear the best way for all men to live in relation to God and to other people. The Ten Commandments, then, are still God's standard for civilised and God-fearing life.

Some Christians have questioned whether the Old Testament command not to murder need cover the mercy-killing of euthanasia. However, the Bible does not distinguish degrees of killing nor motives in the deliberate killing of an innocent person. In all cases the end result is a dead person whose life has been taken by another. The command of God from Genesis through to Jesus is: 'You shall not murder.'

Throughout the books of Israel's history, and in the Psalms and the Prophets, God declares his care for disadvantaged people in society, as we shall see in a later chapter on suffering. So it is no surprise when Jesus declares that we are valued in God's sight for who we are, rather than for what we can contribute; and we are to value others likewise.

'Don't be afraid,' he says. 'You are of more value than many sparrows!'

7

Assisted Suicide

Thus far the main emphasis of our discussion has been on voluntary euthanasia, where the physician terminates the life of the patient who requests it. However, the focus of comment in the United Kingdom is now changing to assisted dying (merely a change in name) and assisted suicide – quite a different matter. We have already met the concept of assisted suicide in our exploration of practice in the Netherlands and, notably, in Oregon State in the United States of America. It is also the method of euthanasia practised most in Switzerland. We are talking about a patient being assisted in committing suicide when he or she could not perform it by him- or herself.

Such a patient was Mr Reginald Crew, whom we met earlier when we were looking at the practice in Switzerland. Here the lethal medication would be mixed in water, dissolved and put in reach of the patient who would drink it.

Assisted suicide carries inherent safeguards that are absent in euthanasia. Notably it ensures that the act is voluntary. The patient has expressed a wish for assistance with suicide. After appropriate questioning and, if the law requires it, after a period of reflection and possibly assessment by a second doctor, a palliative physician and, in some cases, a psychiatrist, and with evidence of a persistent wish, the doctor or assistant provides the potion. Then it is the patient's deliberate action to drink the solution.

Of course, if the patient is physically unable to drink a draught, some other means of self-administration must be found. Ingenious methods have been invented, including a drip into a vein which has to be started by the patient knocking down a small lever which opens the tap.

By these methods the doctor or assistant is merely making possible a legal action – suicide – which the patient was physically unable to perform.

Suicide

So how does the law stand with regard to suicide?

Suicide was decriminalised in the United Kingdom as recently as 1961. Many of today's attempted suicides are interrupted and do not lead to death. They often prove to be 'cries for help' from distressed individuals in misery or depression for different reasons. Perhaps a final end was not anticipated – at least subconsciously – by many of them. The fact is that recent statistics show that there are between 5,000 and 6,000 suicides a year in England and Wales, but there are probably about 170,000 attempted suicides each year.

Formerly, suicide had been regarded as not only a criminal act but also a sinful one – even an unforgivable sin. G. Lloyd Carr (a professor of biblical and theological studies in the USA) has written helpfully on suicide, speaking out of the experience of the suicide of his own son.[1] He reviews Christian teaching from the Bible and the church fathers. He says that the traditional Christian view has followed the teaching of St Augustine in the fifth century AD and Thomas Aquinas in the thirteenth, but there is no specific biblical instruction in this matter. Augustine had quoted the sixth commandment, saying that 'Thou shalt not kill' prohibited killing oneself as much as killing any other person. Aquinas added arguments from natural law and society's expectations, also from the view that all life was from God and only he could reclaim it.

Carr points out that both these thinkers spoke and wrote out of their own time and situation – and it is still true today that we must not make light of suicide or make it easier to contemplate it. Nevertheless, he argues forcefully that neither the Old and New Testaments (where they deal with the few suicides recorded[2]) nor Jewish thinkers have regarded suicide as an unforgivable sin. In fact, we are told in Mark 3:29 that there is only one unforgivable sin, and that is blaspheming the Holy Spirit:

> I tell you the truth, all the sins and blasphemies of men will be forgiven them. But whoever blasphemes against the Holy Spirit will never be forgiven; he is guilty of an eternal sin.

The idea that suicide is unforgivable stems from the fact that between the act and the death there is no time for confession or penance. For the Christian, however, the Bible teaches that we are born (again) out of the state of death into eternal life by grace through faith, and that God is able to keep us in eternal life. Jesus promises that no one can cause to perish those to whom he has given eternal life, for no one can snatch them out of the Father's hand. Paul concludes that neither death nor life will be able to separate us from the love of God that is in Christ Jesus.

While suicide is a terribly final act by which the promise and hope of this life are extinguished, the Bible gives no reason to believe that suicide also extinguishes the hope of eternal life for the believer, a hope which is settled on other criteria.

The British legislators took some of these considerations, and also a changed attitude to morality, into account when they decided to decriminalise suicide in 1961. But they insisted that aiding and abetting a suicide should remain a criminal offence and wrote that into the law.

Assisted suicide

Today some people argue that assisting someone who lacks the physical ability to do what is no longer a criminal act cannot itself be criminal. As a consequence they also ask why it should continue to be criminal for a doctor to prescribe medication, knowing that it will be used for suicide.

Experience with assisted suicide

We remarked that assisted suicide has been legal in the State of Oregon in the USA since 1997. By 2003, 265 prescriptions for a lethal potion had been issued and 117 people had chosen to take the potion. In 2003, assisted suicide accounted for 42 out of 30,000 deaths.

When the observers from the House of Lords' Select Committee visited Oregon they were assured that the Oregon Board of Examiners had not heard of any complications of any significance. They seemed to be aware that rumours were circulating, but had no evidence of problems.[3]

The Nightingale Alliance,[4] however, reports that a general practitioner and professor at Oregon Health Sciences University, Dr Toffler, has commented that 'every case we know about, and it is close to a dozen cases now, has serious problems'. Among those were several people who had suffered from depression but had no psychiatric assessment before the assisted suicide. At least one patient, 43-year-old Patrick Matheny, delayed taking his medication until his disease had advanced to a point where he was unable to adequately swallow and a relative had to help him.

In the Netherlands the Royal Dutch Medical Association and other leading authorities recommend doctors administer physician-assisted suicide rather than euthanasia where possible. However, the rate of physician-assisted suicide remains low – at 2 per 1,000 deaths – against euthanasia at 26 per 1,000, according to the anonymous survey of 2002. The figure of 2 assisted suicides per 1,000 deaths adds up to 280 per year (there were 140,000 deaths in the year 2001).

Problems with assisted suicide

An article in the *New England Journal of Medicine* reports that there have been problems with assisted suicide in the Netherlands, in that some 7 in every 100 have had complications such as vomiting, and that 16 in every 100 failed to come to the desired result, so that lethal injection was required to complete the action in 21 cases out of 114 in 1990–91 and 1995–96.

The evidence indicates three practical problems

encountered. We discover there are patients whose illness progresses beyond where they are able to undertake even assisted suicide. But they have made their decision, have obtained the agreement of the doctor and have the medication. Is it fair for them, after all these preparations, to be unable to complete the action? Secondly, after taking the medication, some suffer complications which need controlling or which may indicate a different prescription. And thirdly, there are some for whom the medication produces a lingering death or does not kill.

In all these cases, Dutch experience shows that the physician has needed to resort to lethal injection – which, of course, requires euthanasia to be legalised, at least for patients where assistance with suicide fails.

Moral and ethical questions

The question remains, does not prescribing a lethal dose of medicine, known to be intended to cause the death of the patient, carry with it responsibility for the death? Is not physician-assisted suicide as much killing a patient as is euthanasia? Where is the moral difference?

Here we are back to the considerations which brought the legislators of the 1961 Suicide Act to specify:

> A person who aids, abets, counsels or procures the suicide of another, or an attempt by another to commit suicide, shall be liable on conviction or indictment to imprisonment for a term not exceeding 14 years.

In principle and practice, then, assisted suicide is merely a variant of voluntary euthanasia. Here, too, someone is agreeing that a person's estimate of their quality of life is so poor that it is no longer worth living, and so they agree to provide the means or ability to terminate that life. With assisted suicide we are again into the arguments of Chapters 2, 3 and 4 about the rightness of someone's terminating or assisting in the termination of another's life.

8

How Long?

It was a quiet Sunday afternoon. I had called in to the hospice to make sure everyone was comfortable. In the bay window of a four-bedded room an elderly gentleman, Wilfred, was seated with two children on his lap listening to their grandad's stories. He was in the hospice because secondary tumours in his liver from his cancer had caused jaundice, and had affected the control of his diabetes. Opposite, his son and daughter-in-law were relaxing against the window post. What a picture for a peaceful Sunday afternoon!

'Hallo,' I said. 'It's good to see the family together. You're very welcome.'

'Thank you,' said the husband. 'But this is all dragging out and it's awful to see Dad suffering so. Can't you do anything to stop the suffering?'

'I'm so sorry,' I said. 'Has the pain started up again?'

'Oh no,' said the son. 'You seem to have that completely under control.'

'Is it the sickness or lack of appetite that is a problem?'

'No, it's not that. Indeed, you have relaxed the restrictions he has had since his diabetes was diagnosed 37 years ago, and he calls the lady who brings the tea the "cake-lady"! No, he seems to be enjoying his food.'

'So what do you mean about the suffering?'

There was a considerable pause. 'Well,' said Wilfred's son thoughtfully, 'I suppose it's really our suffering, seeing him needing to be cared for and not able to get out. No, he is actually enjoying the attention!'

So we will look at what suffering is, and who suffers. We need to note, too, the problem of prolonged suffering. Can there be any benefit to the sufferer from their suffering and should we always try to relieve suffering? And what about treatment that might actually prolong suffering by prolonging the dying? These are some of the questions that Wilfred raises for us in this chapter.

Physical, psychological and spiritual suffering

Wilfred's pain had been relieved. There had been very real physical pain, nausea and sickness, and he had totally lost his appetite before he came into the hospice. Some of these problems – or 'symptoms' – had been dealt with at home by his family doctor, who had given appropriate drugs to settle his pain and sickness. We had had little to change in his medication. When he came to us, the problem had been loneliness and the insecurity of wondering what would happen if something went badly wrong at night or at the weekend when he was on his own. Much of his suffering – like that of so many people – had been psychological and social in origin. Not that the family did not care. They came to visit and provide support as often as they could, and Dad always declared that he valued his independence.

But we are whole people, not bodies separate from our minds and spirits. Anxiety, loneliness, fear and depression are all aspects of human suffering. Just as these feelings can have deep effects on our physical well-being, so our physical ailments affect our mind and spirit.

And, of course, our spiritual peacefulness or otherwise has implications for body and mind. And this was what Wilfred's son and daughter-in-law needed to discover as they watched and listened to their father and his grandchildren. They were suffering from the waiting in anticipation of their ultimate loss. Wilfred, however, had found peacefulness in the calm and company of the hospice. He had also responded to the spiritual peace which so often goes with a place where prayer is made or which is supported by prayer.

Prolonged suffering

Some of the most difficult pains to relieve are those that have been present for a long time before the painkillers are started. The same is true of other symptoms. Acute pain is often associated with anxiety, but when the symptoms are prolonged and unrelieved they become debilitating and depressing. Such depression is communicated unintentionally to carers and visitors, so that the attempt to support and care becomes the more difficult and itself depressing.

This is the sort of situation which leads to demands for euthanasia.

On the other hand, prolonged suffering does not necessarily lead to depression. Daisy was in her late 80s. She lived with two sisters and a brother in the rented family house until well into her 70s. She was invariably cheerful and was a support to many people around her. When the weather was damp she used to remark from time to time that the 'screws' were troublesome, but she never complained. Later she went into a residential home, maintaining her cheerfulness, and became a source of peace and content-ment in the home. She used to hobble dreadfully and it was evident that her feet and legs were a problem. 'Yes, dear, the screws are a bit of a trouble today,' was the nearest to a complaint that I ever heard. Even when she had to be moved to a nursing home and then became progressively more disabled, she continued to care for others in a won-derfully selfless way.

Medically, she had advanced arthritis – and I suspect that it was basically rheumatoid arthritis which had led on to osteoarthritis. It must have been very painful. At the same time she was supporting her younger sister and their unmarried brother who had learning difficulties and was never in regular employment, but who had lived with them all his life. But the social constraints in this family never limited their cheerfulness or commitment to each other and to neighbours and friends who needed their help. Daisy would say that her secret was a deep trust in the love and providence of God. She maintained a wide correspondence with people all over the world and her prayer lists for her many 'friends' were extensive!

Prolonged dying

Daisy remained very much alive till her last hours. Sadly, for some people dying is prolonged over weeks or months.

This was the situation of Tony Bland, who was crushed in the Hillsborough Stadium disaster and whose brain never recovered. His parents watched what seemed to them to be a living death for more than three years. We spoke about persistent vegetative state in Chapter 5; here we need to note the difficulty that people have when their death or that of their loved one is greatly delayed (as they see it) or drawn out. The suffering of the patient may be great; that of the family – such as Wilfred's son and daughter-in-law – may seem even greater.

Tony Bland and the persistent vegetative state

In 1989 a young man, Tony Bland, was crushed in a stampede at a football match at the Hillsborough Stadium in Sheffield. He was resuscitated but his brain had suffered disastrous oxygen starvation. It appeared that the higher centres had been irretrievably damaged but the brain stem continued to function so that Tony was able to breathe normally, although he could not feed himself or communicate. He was in what is called the persistent vegetative state.

After more than two years with no progress, his parents wanted Tony to be released from his increasingly twisted body, and his family doctor believed that the feeding tube should be removed so that Tony could be allowed to die. Other authorities believed that that would open the parents and the hospital to a serious risk of criminal liability. The matter was pursued through the courts to the House of Lords, where the law lords accepted the wishes of the parents and the doctor and allowed the removal of the feeding tube. Tony Bland died in March 1993.

There remains uncertainty as to whether this was the first case of legally sanctioned euthanasia in the United Kingdom, or simply the allowing of the completion of delayed death caused by the original accident.

Indeed, I used to be surprised to receive occasional requests for euthanasia from relatives rather than from the person who was actually dying. It now seems to me that the closer the relationship to the dying person the less likely people are to request hastening of the process.

Nevertheless, a protracted period of slow deterioration of body or mind is very difficult to watch or experience. It is very difficult to hear some of our hospice patients say, 'Why does God not take me? I'm ready to go, and I pray every night that I will not wake up.' So we must ask whether any benefit can possibly be drawn from this experience, and, indeed, from suffering itself.

What does the Bible say about suffering?

The apostle Paul knew a great deal about suffering. During his missionary journeys he records for us something of the extent of the sufferings he experienced.

> I've worked much harder, been jailed more often, beaten up more times than I can count, and at death's door time after time. I've been flogged five times with the Jews' thirty-nine lashes, beaten by Roman rods three times, pummelled with rocks once. I've been shipwrecked three times, and immersed

in the open sea for a night and a day. In hard travelling year in and year out, I've had to ford rivers, fend off robbers, struggle with friends, struggle with foes. I've been at risk in the city, at risk in the country, endangered by desert sun and sea storm, and betrayed by those I thought were my brothers. I've known drudgery and hard labour, many a long and lonely night without sleep, many a missed meal, blasted by the cold, naked to the weather . . . (2 Corinthians 11:23–27, *The Message*)

Indeed he says that after the Lord Jesus appeared to him in the vision on the Damascus Road, the Lord said to Ananias, 'I will show him how much he must suffer for my name.'

Paul says that he believes that suffering can, as it were, strengthen our mettle as Christians:

We also rejoice in our sufferings, because we know that suffering produces perseverance; perseverance, character; and character, hope. And hope does not disappoint us, because God has poured out his love into our hearts by the Holy Spirit, whom he has given us. (Romans 5:3–5)

We have known people who have grown spiritually during their period of suffering and for whom the last days have given opportunity for a new or deepened commitment. What a tragedy if those days had been shortened by human action!

I think of a very senior nurse whom I met in a busy and noisy intensive neurosurgical ward. Operation for a brain tumour had been followed by blood clotting in both legs and one of those clots breaking off and ending up in her lungs. She was very ill, confused and restless. It was evident that she was dying and that this ward was not the right place for her care. I was able to have her transferred to a hospice bed at once, and went to see her there a little while after the ambulance journey.

My usual practice was to sit on the bed as I talked with patients, and I went to do so. Through the haze of confusion from pain-relief medication and illness emerged the senior nurse: 'Are there no chairs in the hospice, doctor?' she asked! During the next few days 'Julia' became clear in her thinking and enjoyed the presence of her sister, who visited frequently. Nevertheless, her illness progressed.

A few days later, on my arrival in the hospice one morning, I was told that our friend had been particularly restless the previous night. Someone had sat with her, which had helped for a while. Later in response to a request, one of the nurses had taken her to the chapel and read through the morning prayer. That, too, had helped for a while. But she was still crying out: would I go and see her?

Julia seemed very muddled and only partially coherent. But a few words came through clearly, notably 'guilt' and 'forgiveness'. It was shortly before Good Friday and quietly I spoke with her of Jesus' death in our place, to gain for us the forgiveness of God. She seemed very receptive and I took the (for me) unusual step of leading a prayer of commitment to Jesus and asked him to give her a sense of his forgiveness and of peace. Certainly the restlessness and anxiety disappeared and never returned.

Julia died very gently three days later. On the next day her sister returned to collect the death certificate and her belongings. She thanked me for all we had done. On the day before Julia died she had spoken of the comfort she had gained and said how she wished that her sister, too, might come into this place of peace that she had found. No, not

the hospice, but the place of forgiveness and security with
her God.

Comforting others

Paul has another insight to share with us about suffering. In
the second letter to the Corinthians he has a lot to say about
the comfort he received from God in his sufferings. It has
given him something to share with others in their distress.
He thanks God, 'the Father of compassion and God of all
comfort, who comforts us in all our troubles, so that we can
comfort those in any trouble with the comfort we ourselves
have received from God' (2 Corinthians 1:3–4).

Yes, that, too, is a benefit which the sufferer is sometimes
able to pass on. We spoke of Daisy earlier. That was exactly
Daisy's gift to many, and we have known others, often elderly, frail folk, who are a blessing to the visitor. They share
with us out of the richness of their experience of comfort in
their need, and that provides strength to healthy visitors,
many of whom have their own troubles.

Sharing in Christ's sufferings

There is a third benefit – no, rather, privilege – which comes
to Christians unexpectedly and perhaps mysteriously as a
result of their suffering. In the letter to the Philippians, dic-
tated by Paul while chained and in a Roman prison (not a
pleasant place in first-century Rome), he speaks of his great
aim in life:

> I want to know Christ and the power of his resurrection and
> the fellowship of sharing in his sufferings, becoming like him

in his death, and so, somehow, to attain to the resurrection
from the dead. (Philippians 3:10–11)

The order of these phrases seems to be an anticlimax. To
start with knowing the power of Christ's resurrection, and
then to aim to become like him in his death, by way of sharing in his sufferings, seems inverted progress. And it is! But
that was Jesus' way – to turn the priorities of the world
upside-down. So Paul believed that his present sufferings
were worth bearing, as a sharing in the sufferings of Christ.
Indeed, he dares to say of them, 'I rejoice in what was suffered for you, and I fill up in my flesh what is still lacking in
regard to Christ's afflictions, for the sake of his body, which
is the church' (Colossians 1:24). The New Testament
assures us that Christ has undergone all that is necessary for
our reconciliation with God, but nevertheless our sufferings
help to complete the picture. To see that our suffering puts
us at one with Christ in his service of mankind is an unexpected privilege indeed!

Relief of suffering

Am I saying it is so blessed to suffer that we should not try
to relieve suffering, or to give medication to diminish suffering?

Of course not. In the Old Testament passage about Moses
and the burning bush, God says, 'I have indeed seen the
misery of my people . . . I have heard them crying out . . .
and I am concerned about their suffering. So I have come
down to rescue them . . .'(Exodus 3:7–8). God himself
makes plain to Moses that he is not content that his people

continue to live in suffering and distress, but that he himself will do what is necessary to rescue them – and in this instance he will use Moses for the purpose. It is also worth noting that, as often in the Bible's accounts, God uses a human agent to bring about relief of suffering.

We have noticed that Paul in 2 Corinthians 1 speaks about the comfort he has received in his sufferings. Again, in the letter to the Philippians he speaks of receiving help in his sufferings, this time (and frequently) from the church in Philippi (Philippians 4:10–16). Earlier in the letter he has spoken of the mutual care and concern the church and his fellow workers have had for one another, sent and received through their messenger, Epaphroditus. He himself had become very sick while bringing help to Paul and the church in Philippi had shown their love and concern for him, too (Philippians 2:25–28).

We have already noticed that Jesus himself was grateful for fluid to relieve his thirst on the cross, and was willing to receive the wine-vinegar at the end (Mark 15:36; John 19:28–30), perhaps a mild analgesic. So he himself authorises our use of people and medications for the relief of suffering.

Prolonging of suffering

There is one final question we should look at in this chapter. While we see it is right to seek to relieve suffering, should we – and do we sometimes – give treatment that will prolong suffering?

This is one of the big problems in modern medicine. With our sophisticated medical techniques for life support and the increasingly powerful antibiotics and other medications, doctors are often able to protect living people, but also to prolong their dying. One of the big ethical dilemmas doctors and healthcare staff face today is the question of when to give and when to withhold treatment.

Among the principles that govern medical practice are:

- a good knowledge of the effects and side effects of drugs
- good communication skills for sharing that knowledge
- skill in balancing potential benefit and harm
- awareness and acceptance of the patient's wishes
- time given to explaining issues to patients and their carers.

We seek to respect patients' rights to make their own decisions regarding treatment. That includes the right to refuse treatment if they believe the burden of that treatment to be too great. Some people are unable to make their wishes known at the critical time; perhaps because they are unconscious from accident or injury. Then the decisions will rest with the carer – either the person's next of kin, or the medical staff dealing with the incident. Under these circumstances it is helpful if the person has declared their wishes in advance – through an 'advance directive' – and we shall look at this in a later chapter.

Medical treatment is generally 'iterative'; that is, decisions proceed stepwise. A diagnosis is made; tests are performed; then actions are started that are aimed to cure or ameliorate the situation. The response of the patient and his condition are watched, further decisions are made in the light of the test results and the patient's responses, further actions are taken, and so on. These responses include acknowledgement of the patient's wishes as well as his physical condition. This means that the medical staff should be willing to withdraw treatments which are perceived by the patient as being too burdensome. But withdrawing treatment is never an easy decision – and we shall come to this in our next chapter. It also means that, at every stage, the patient should be at liberty to say, 'That's enough: please stop the treatment.'

In summary, we have looked at some of the issues raised by the suffering of patients and their carers. Of course there is much more that we could have explored. Where does suffering come from? Why does suffering exist and how can it be squared with a God who is both all-good and all-powerful? And so on. Books have been written about these matters and the Bible faces them squarely as it tells the story of God's dealings with people.

But we have tried to look specifically at the issues of suffering in 'whole people', whether patient or carer; at whether God, through the Bible, can point to any benefits in our characters from suffering; and whether God's intention, the prevention or relief of our suffering, can be mirrored in our medical actions and care.

9

Of Tablets, Tests and Tubes

It was a pleasant dinner reunion with old friends. We had not met for some years, but had kept in touch through various adventures of life. So we 'set the world to rights', as they say, and then talked about our families. Cheryl's dad, it appeared, had been wandering, mentally as well as physically, due to Alzheimer's, and the situation had been getting worse. Now he had suffered a stroke and had had to go into a nursing home: how he hated leaving his own home! Our friends had been distressed by the change in him – he hardly knew them – and clearing the squalor into which his flat had descended was awful. He had obviously been very ill, but his pneumonia had responded to antibiotics temporarily, although there was little improvement in his physical and mental state. Now, however, the chest infection had returned and the carers were talking about yet more treatment. 'Surely you wouldn't treat him with more antibiotics?' said our friends.

Where have we heard this before?

The question of when to withhold treatment during the late stages of a person's life is never easy. Where patient, family and professionals hold the same opinion, such decisions are made much easier in a meeting together. But what, we may ask, are the guiding principles behind such decisions, and who should make them? Incidentally, these days the person closest to a patient may not be a blood or marriage relation, but for our purposes in this chapter, we shall include all such in the term 'family'.

Who decides?

The General Medical Council has given doctors guidance regarding this sort of decision-making, and I have found it helpful to refer to their booklet in preparation of this chapter.[1]

Ultimately, in the UK, the doctor can advise and is responsible for prescribing any medications, but the patient is the one who decides whether to seek advice, to take the advice, and to swallow any prescribed medication. Responsibility rests with him or her, assuming they are mentally capable of making those decisions (in legal terms, 'competent to decide'). A problem arises, however, if the patient is unconscious or mentally incapable of deciding rationally ('incompetent').

Provision is now available for a person to express directions as to how they wish to be treated under such circumstances, and we shall be exploring these advance directives in the next chapter. In the absence of an applicable advance directive, decisions must be made by the treating doctor, the caring team and the 'family' of the patient. Again, the ultimate responsibility for prescribing rests with the doctor, but he would be wise to have sought the views of carers and family.

To treat or not to treat?

These are days (in some parts of the world, it must be said) of increasingly powerful medications, of drips and tubes, and of life-support machines, as well as efficient techniques of resuscitation. So much so that we have been tempted to think that death can be indefinitely postponed; or, if it happens, must be a consequence of negligence. Of course, the truth is that we are still mortal and that death does come to each of us in the natural course of events. What most of us would prefer to avoid is a prolonged dying with diminished mental and physical faculties. Can we know that all necessary will be done for us; but that when the time comes we shall be able to go in peace?

Mr Leslie Burke: stopping administration of food and fluids?

Mr Leslie Burke is a gentleman who suffers from a progressive degenerative disease called spino-cerebellar ataxia. He was anxious that he might reach the point where he was dependent on food and fluids administered by tube or drip ('artificial hydration and nutrition' is the medical term) but could no longer communicate his wishes. It might be that his doctors would decide that his condition was too poor to continue the food and fluid and might allow him to die of starvation and thirst. In July 2004 he brought a case against the guidance established by the General Medical Council (GMC) in the belief that his human rights might be breached. The judge declared the GMC guidance unlawful in some respects.

However, a High Court appeal in July 2005 established

that the GMC guidance was lawful, but that it did not allow doctors to discontinue artificial nutrition and hydration from any patient who, when competent, had declared a wish to be kept alive by those means. 'Any doctor who deliberately brings that patient's life to an end by discontinuing the supply of artificial nutrition and hydration will not merely be in breach of duty but guilty of murder,' said Lord Phillips, Master of the Rolls and head of the three appeal judges. However, Lord Phillips added that in the last stage of life artificial nutrition and hydration might not prolong life but might even hasten death. At this point whether to provide it was a clinical decision for the doctor.

The President of the General Medical Council commented, 'We have always said that causing patients to die from starvation and dehydration is absolutely unacceptable practice and unlawful.'[2]

Medical practice and the law agree that respect for life is a primary responsibility, but that it is right to avoid burdening people with unnecessary, intrusive or unwanted treatment 'just because it is there'. There is always a balance to be struck between the benefits and the burdens of treatment. Side effects of medicines are common and the wise physician learns to ask whether a person wants yet more pills to swallow, with the risk of nausea, diarrhoea and so on, if they are not absolutely necessary or if the person is nearing the end of life. It is perfectly legal and ethical for the doctor to withhold treatments that will be too burdensome, or to withdraw such treatments once started.

So, in the case of Cheryl's dad, we hope the doctor will examine him – and ensure that he can express his own opinion if possible – and then talk with the nursing home staff and the family if they are available. Then he will decide whether to give antibiotics or other treatment. But we also hope he will not lay the burden of decision too strongly on the shoulders of the family, even the nearest and dearest. I remember talking about these decisions with the staff of a psychiatric hospital and a senior consultant supported this emphatically. Another consultant had asked him whether he wanted his own father to have antibiotic treatment for a potentially terminal chest infection, and he had found it very painful to have to make such a decision for his own parent.

We need to be reminded, too, that people have recovered from chest infections, including pneumonia, before anti-biotics were discovered, and that others have died from pneumonia even while being treated with them. Death and cure do not hang entirely on our, or the doctor's, decisions!

Are such decisions affected by the presence of an under-lying incurable condition such as cancer, a stroke, dementia or AIDS? Yes and no. Some of these conditions have a nat-urally up-and-down pattern, and if we can help the person through a patch of worsened illness we can hope for another period of acceptable life quality. This is often the case in AIDS, and with some cancers. People with AIDS have often been through such episodes before and may want maximum treatment: they know that in the past they have been at death's door and have recovered; so why not this time?

Recovery from a stroke is often slow and may reach a

point of no improvement, when pneumonia may worsen the outlook considerably. In dementia, again, the condition may become significantly worse after an infection. However, each person responds in a different way, and so needs to be treated as an individual. Where the symptoms of an infection are distressing, the use of antibiotics to relieve distress is often appropriate.

What about food?

Provision of food and fluids is a different matter from medical treatment. Of course, even basically healthy people need to go without food at times – when they have an upset stomach, for example. But most times our instinct is to provide food, and to encourage people to eat. 'You've got to keep your strength up,' we say. We acknowledge that very ill people cannot stomach a three-course meal, and we offer light foods. Our hospices have developed a particular skill in attractively presenting small nourishing meals for very sick people, as far as possible to the patient's own desires.

However, there often comes a time when the patient refuses to eat, despite encouragement and attractive presentation. Then what? The nurses' answer is to persist with offering attractive food, and gently persuading, but – as we saw with Jim in Chapter 1 – they have to accept that we cannot force patients to eat against their will. Neither is it good for people to have food forced into their mouths in severe illness. In advanced cancer the disease itself may make it impossible for the body to absorb foodstuffs – hence the weight loss and emaciation. So to force food against what a person feels able to tolerate might only feed the cancer, rather than the person. How often we have to explain this, and persuade relatives not to force their loved one to struggle!

Sometimes, during a person's severe illness, a tube has been inserted through the nose or the tummy wall to allow feeding when disease has prevented them from swallowing. We occasionally do this when a cancer is blocking the gullet, or when a nerve weakness (such as motor neurone disease [MND], or a stroke) blocks the swallowing mechanism. Can it be right at some stage to stop the tube-feeding, and how can we decide when?

Again, a conscious and aware person may simply tell us that he or she feels the time has come when the feeding is burdensome and not helpful. People should be allowed the right to make their own decision; this is the autonomy about which we spoke in Chapter 2. It is more difficult with an unconscious person, but it may become obvious to the medical attendants that the food is producing bloating of the tummy, bowel troubles and perhaps sickness, and that the tummy should be rested. We can then replace food with fluid and reduce distress.

Some years ago I was asked to see a 50-year-old patient in hospital who had suffered two strokes affecting both sides of his body. He was conscious but totally unable to move anything. He was being lovingly and skilfully cared for by the nurses and was being fed through a tube through his nose. One night the tube had come out. The nurses had replaced it. The next night the same thing happened and it had been replaced. During the next week the tube came out three more times. How, no one ever knew, though it was suspected that he himself had rejected his tube. And the nurses who knew him best said that every time they went to replace the tube his eyes said, 'Please don't put it back.' Should it continue to be replaced? His condition was incurable. His distress was obvious. He could be kept pain-free and prevented from getting dehydrated by other means. Perhaps not replacing the tube would be the right way forward. Such decisions are never easy and are usually best made in discussion with the professional caring team and the family, as we have said before, and always trying to ascertain the patient's wishes in the matter.

And withdrawal of fluids?

Even more difficult is the question of whether doctors should ever withdraw or withhold fluids from a patient. Asked like that, the response seems obvious: no. And yet it is not quite so simple.

Ellen was in her 90s. She had fallen and broken her hip. At the local hospital the doctors had pinned the break and she was sitting out and had begun to walk – but reluctantly! One morning she was just curled up on her side. She had apparently refused any breakfast; at least, it had remained untouched. No drinks during the morning, and now nothing at lunchtime. She had been taking less and less over the previous two days (which had been a weekend), said the nurses. As a doctor, I decided she needed a drip, and set one up with difficulty. The very experienced ward sister came along during the procedure and asked, 'Does everyone have to have a drip in order to die, doctor?' How right was her unspoken inference, because just two hours later Ellen passed on and I had learned an important lesson.

It would not have been negligence to have allowed Ellen to go without fluids. Indeed it was probably misdirected and invasive care to have set up the drip. For Ellen, the time had simply come, and she did not need the interference.

But how do we know when that time is?

Sometimes the patient knows and can tell us or refuse intervention. Often they simply stop responding to suggestions that they have another drink or sip of fluid. Sometimes family or carers are aware that the time has come. But often we have to discourage the relatives from giving too much fluid; they can help a great deal by moistening their loved one's lips with a small sponge dipped in water on which the patient can suck if he or she wishes.

Is there a problem with giving fluid by drip at this stage? People are often surprised not to see more drips for patients dying in hospice. That is partly because people are encouraged to take fluid by mouth whenever possible, and all the staff give time to encouraging the next sip. But it is also because the patient's failing heart or lungs can easily be overloaded with fluid at this late stage in life, resulting in fluid on the lungs, in the legs, uncomfortable swelling of the stomach or even swelling of the brain of the recumbent person. This is particularly true if that part is affected by a growth.

What about people getting 'dehydrated'? We all know that in a desert you have to have water! But we are not talking about people in tropical heat where the situation is very different, nor should a hospice bed be equated with dehydration when crossing the Sahara!

Of course there are times when it is perfectly appropriate to set up a drip for a patient, to allow fluid to run into a vein or, slowly, under the skin. But on the whole, people who feel dry are willing to drink at least a little, or to sip from the sponge. They take enough to keep the mouth moist – which is enough to prevent feelings of thirst – until they no longer need the intervention, and we can allow them to be free of encumbrances for their last journey.

A final thought

People ask about providing food, fluid and medications during advanced illness. The Lord Jesus reminded us of another dimension. 'Man does not live by bread alone, but by every word that comes from the mouth of God,' he said, quoting a teaching of centuries earlier (Matthew 4:4, quoting Deuteronomy 8:3).

Some of our patients have found the reassurance and strength that comes from confidence in the teachings of the Scripture and prayer. We should not underestimate the value of loved words from the Bible, such as the Psalms, to seriously ill people. The assurance of the presence and love of the Lord is a very great help to many.

10

Planning Ahead

The last chapter began with someone suffering from the dementia caused by Alzheimer's disease. Sadly, as age increases, so does the frequency of the progressive conditions which result in loss of memory (mainly memory for recent events or information – called short-term memory loss). With this goes difficulty in making decisions – or at least in communicating them. So a person like my friend's dad loses the 'competence' to control his life, including such matters as the place where he will be cared for, and the extent to which medical intervention should be prolonged. Is the length of life or its quality the more important to him at this stage? If and when it comes to life-prolonging treatment, the doctors and nurses who care for him need to know what he would want.

Doctor knows best

Until recently, it was generally accepted that the doctors knew most about all the options, and could be trusted to

makf   the attitude of many
pe⁄   ers to their doctors or
⁄   al pros and cons. How-
                                              ese important decisions
⁄   , the Internet for the lat-
                                              ı they really be sure that
⁄⁄ℓ   ⌐⌐₃ ·   isions for them, seeing it
from their point of view?

That may be fine while we are competent, but can we make provision for how we are treated if we are no longer able to communicate?

The answer is 'yes and no'! In this chapter we explore advance directives (the so-called living wills), which provide us with a means for declaring in advance how we wish to be treated under particular circumstances. But we shall see that even they cannot necessarily reflect our minds when the unexpected actually occurs.

What are advance directives?

The advance directive is a document stating how we wish to be treated under certain circumstances if we are no longer competent to express our wishes. It is carefully drawn up, signed and witnessed, and deposited with people who are likely to be involved in making decisions for us: our family doctor (GP), our solicitor, and our next of kin or other carer. It is wise to involve a solicitor in drawing up the advance directive (as we normally would in drawing up a will), and it should certainly be discussed with our GP or other medical attendant and the carer or family member who will be responsible for seeing that it is acted upon.

Types of advance statement[1]

- **Advance directive**: The patient refuses a particular treatment or procedure. This is legally binding.
- **Specifying directive**: The patient can specify the degree of irreversible mental and physical deterioration after which no life-sustaining treatment should be given. This is legally binding.
- **Requesting statement**: The patient lists aspirations and treatment preferences. This is for information and is not legally binding.
- **Statement of beliefs and values**: The patient lists his or her relevant religious and moral values. This is for information and is not legally binding.
- **Naming statement**: The patient names another person who should be consulted at the time a decision has to be made. This is for information and is not legally binding.

Some or all of these may be combined.

You will find an example of an advance directive on pages 129–131, and we will be referring to that example here. There are a number of other models available.

In drawing up an advance directive, we define the principles that we wish to use to guide decisions. For instance, do we want all possible treatment to preserve our life, even if disabled; or do we want to be allowed to die with treatment solely to preserve comfort? In our example, the person indicates that, for her, actions are to be based on her fear of degeneration and indignity rather than a fear of death. For another person, on the other hand, length of life might be the important consideration.

The circumstances we define should be wide enough to cover all, or at least most, eventualities. The directive should avoid ambiguities as these may delay institution of appropriate treatment, but it must allow for unforeseen events. So declaring a refusal to accept surgery in the event of advanced cancer, for example, might prevent appropriate treatment for a limb fractured coincidentally. In the example we quote, the person defines a list of progressive or disabling conditions under which she would wish the directive to be enacted. The schedule of such conditions is clear and, within her intentions, comprehensive.

There are limits to what can be specified. We cannot specify anything that would be illegal; thus, unless the law is changed, we cannot ask for euthanasia in the advance directive. Neither can the doctor be required to give treatment that he believes to be unnecessary or ineffectual. It would obviously be a waste of money and potentially scarce resources if doctors were to be obliged to give expensive treatments that would inevitably be ineffective. And thus the law recognises that doctors, too, should have their autonomy respected.

Does the advance directive have to be observed? Yes, the comments on types of directives on page 127 indicate that an advance directive contains elements which are legally binding and other elements which indicate how a person wants his thinking respected. Provided the doctor has had his attention drawn to an advance directive, he is expected to work within it. We shall have more to say about this proviso.

Example of an advance directive
(used with permission)

TO MY FAMILY, MY PHYSICIAN AND ALL OTHER PER-
SONS CONCERNED THIS DIRECTIVE is made by me, . . .
[name] of . . . [address] at a time when I am sound of
mind and after careful consideration,

I DECLARE that if at any time the following circumstances exist namely:
1. I suffer from one or more conditions mentioned in
the schedule; and
2. I have become unable to participate effectively in
decisions about my medical care; and
3. Two independent physicians (one a consultant) are
of the opinion that I am unlikely to recover from
illness or impairment involving serious distress or
incapacity for rational existence,

THEN IN THOSE CIRCUMSTANCES my directions are as
follows:
1. That I am not to be subjected to any medical intervention or treatment aimed at prolonging or sustaining my life;
2. That any distressing symptoms (including any
caused by lack of food or fluid) are to be fully controlled by appropriate analgesic or other treatment
even though the treatment may shorten my life.

I consent to anything proposed to be done or omitted in
compliance with the directions expressed above and

absolve my medical attendants from any civil liability arising out of such acts or omissions.

I wish to be understood that I fear degeneration and indignity far more than I fear death. I ask my medical attendants to bear this statement in mind when considering what my intentions would be in any uncertain situation.

I RESERVE the right to revoke this DIRECTIVE at any time but unless I do so it should be taken to represent my continuing directions.

SCHEDULE

   A Advanced disseminated malignant disease
   B Severe immune deficiency
   C Advanced degenerative disease of the nervous system
   D Severe and lasting brain damage due to injury stroke disease or other causes
   E Senile or presenile dementia whether Alzheimer's multi-infarct or other
   F Any other condition of comparable gravity

Signed . . . .

Date . . . .

WE TESTIFY that the above named signed this Directive in our presence and made it clear to us that she understood what it meant. We do not know of any pressure being brought on her to make such a directive and we believe it was made by her own wish. So far as we are aware we do not stand to gain from her death

Witnessed by

Signature . . . . Signature . . . .
Name . . . . Name . . . .
Address . . . . Address . . . .

Difficulties with advance directives

There are two main difficulties with advance directives: knowing what circumstances are going to arise; and knowing how we will feel at the time. We need to spend a little while looking at these.

You will notice that, in the example in the box, the person has identified a comprehensive list of conditions under which the directive should come into force. Yet she has had to add a 'catch-all' phrase to allow for unforeseen circumstances: 'Any other condition of comparable gravity'. This in itself might create uncertainty at a critical time. The doctor may ask if a given circumstance would be of 'comparable gravity' in the mind of the person if she had become, for example, unconscious and therefore an 'incompetent' sufferer, needing decisions to be made. Ultimately, where we cannot foresee, all we can do is to indicate the principles on which decisions are to be made.

But how do we know how we shall feel in circumstances we have never experienced before? A gentleman suffered a severe medical event while away from home. He was taken to a hospital and resuscitated. It was obvious that he had had a stroke and recovery was slow, but he did recover his speech, and his thinking was unimpaired. Relatives were informed and came as soon as possible. On arriving, they informed the doctors of his advance directive, which stated that he should not be resuscitated if he suffered a stroke.

A week or so later, when he was recovered enough to allow discussion, the doctors explained that they had not known of the advance directive, but in the light of it they must ask what should be done if he should suffer a second similar incident. 'Oh, I would want to be resuscitated,' he said. 'Life is sweet, even if I'm disabled.'

In practice, we find it very difficult to imagine what the reality would be like, living with a disability.

Can an advance directive be changed?

How irrevocable is an advance directive? The statement can be changed at any time, but changes will, of course, have to be sent to all who hold copies of the directive. Indeed, the Law Commission has advised that advance directives can only become legally binding if:

- the patient has expressed a firm decision in full knowledge of the choices and complete understanding of the treatment implications, and
- if the health worker is sure that the advance directive is an up-to-date, valid reflection of the patient's wishes and is applicable to the circumstances.

Responsibilities

Whether or not an advance directive is acted upon depends on a relative or carer who knows about the directive bringing it to the notice of the treating doctor. While it is right that the GP is involved in the drawing up of the directive, it is often going to be a hospital doctor who will need to act upon it. That doctor may be called to treat the person in the Accident and Emergency Department as a medical emergency, or perhaps be required to break bad news of an unexpected diagnosis.

Neither can be expected to guess that an advance directive has been made, but they will need to know about the directive before starting emergency or invasive treatment. Responsibility must rest with the patient's representative – close friend or family member – to let the treating doctor know that an advance directive exists.

Are advance directives useful?

Will the advance directive affect medical practice?

Certainly, if the doctor is aware of the existence (and provisions) of the directive, he or she must obey its requirements.

Insofar as medical practice is genuinely concerned with the patient's well-being and best interests, the directive may make little difference because the caring doctor will try to do the best for his patient anyway.

This certainly used to be the major complaint: 'They are only telling us what a good doctor would do anyway, and it reflects badly on the medical profession that we have to be instructed to do our best.' However, nowadays, when very powerful interventions can be pressed into service to prolong life for extremely poorly people, a particular patient may view an intervention differently from how the doctor sees it.

So it can be very helpful to know whether a particular person wants every possible intervention, or wishes instead to be allowed to die with a minimum of treatments.

11

Alternatives

Every year, millions of people around the world living with a terminal illness suffer unnecessary pain and distress, either unaware of or unable to access the care they need. Good quality hospice and palliative care, which aims to meet the needs of the whole person, can and does provide an answer. This is an issue that affects literally everybody on this planet – we would all like our lives to end peacefully and comfortably. (Archbishop Desmond Tutu, 2005)

It is all very well putting the arguments, whether theoretical or practical, for and against euthanasia; but what should we do for people who are suffering at the end of their lives? What are the practical alternatives; and how can we enable people to live with dignity to the end of their lives? And while we are about it, Archbishop Desmond Tutu reminds us that the need is not only in Britain, or the West: 'This is an issue that affects literally everybody on this planet. . .'

Help the Hospices puts the issue on a big canvas when it reminds us that worldwide over 50 million people die each year. Of these, 80% die in the developing world and many have no access to pain control or even the most basic care.

It is estimated that 60% would benefit from palliative care. We must come back to those statistics, representing millions of individuals like you and me, but in the meantime let us narrow the canvas again. We will concentrate on the situation in the United Kingdom.

Care in the United Kingdom

What is the experience of care for people with advanced progressive and incurable illness in the UK? What alternatives are there to enable the remaining days, weeks and months to be valuable to them? How might we improve the support and care we do provide at the end of life? To focus our ideas we might return to an elderly lady we referred to earlier.

Mabel was elderly, frail and forgetful. She had a number of ailments that were reflected in her 90 years: arthritis and back problems; fluid retention because of a chronic failing heart; sensitivity of the bladder and difficulty in controlling the waterworks. Perhaps the worst problem from her point of view was her failing memory. She had been used to remembering things for all the family; now to be aware that she frequently could not remember the most basic matters was extremely distressing.

Her husband, Joe, was in his 80s and also had heart problems, but was alert and able to manage the home and provide care. He was able to drive and to get both of them to the local church most Sundays – they loved to practise their faith, and found the support and friendship of the minister and many of the church members an enormous help. They also had a very good family doctor whom they had known since moving to the area ten years before. He saw them in the surgery at intervals over the years and mobilised hospital referral when necessary. However, little could be done for Mabel's physical or mental deterioration.

Both of them wanted to remain at home, and Joe used to say that he had taken on a responsibility 60 years earlier 'to love and to cherish till death us do part'. His GP supported that by regular home visits when they could no longer get to the surgery, and he also ensured visits from the district nurses. Various adaptations of the home were possible – fortunately they had moved into a bungalow when they came to the area – and the community occupational therapist gave guidance about available aids. The GP used a variety of medications to keep them both as well as possible, but he also said to them both that when the situation became too difficult to manage at home he would try to get Mabel into a suitable nursing home.

The doctor was as good as his word. Some months later, after a particularly difficult night (Mabel required the loo nine times in five hours and Joe had to help her in and out of bed each time), the GP saw that enough was enough. Within a short time Mabel was admitted to a local nursing home where she was well cared for. Despite Joe's spending much time with her, however, Mabel longed to return home; but that had become impossible. However, the issue of euthanasia no longer seemed to be troubling her; at least, she made no more reference to it. Some six weeks later, Mabel developed a chest infection and very gently and peacefully deteriorated over a few days and died with Joe at her bedside.

Joe seemed to be doing well now. He managed on his

own, visited family, continued to drive and kept the home clean and tidy. Then, exactly three months later, during the church service that he was attending, he just slid sideways in the seat, and died – 'was called Home', as his minister said.

Yes, people can get support as good as that, and for many that will be their experience of care in the community. Unfortunately, this is not the case for everyone. So in this chapter we need to examine possible places of care; availability of skills in care; and, for all, the cost of care.

Place of care

Broadly, there are four options as to place of care in Britain: home with support; nursing home; a hospital bed (in the acute hospital, in intermediate care or for the long-term); or a hospice. Each has its advantages and disadvantages, and the ideal is for each person to be where he or she wishes.

Home

When people are asked where they would wish to be cared for during the late stage of an illness, most say they would want to be at home. Today, as Mabel illustrated for us, much can be done or provided to make staying at home possible. Not only is it the preferred option for most people, it is also the most economical, even when adaptations have to be made and support provided.

Physical supports vary from an extra banister rail and a raised toilet seat to through-ceiling lifts and piped oxygen. People can be provided with aids from walking sticks to electric wheelchairs, and from deaf-aids to Light-Writers (used when speech has failed). Amazing adaptations can be made possible with electronic devices to support people whose strength in arms and legs has gone. We are constantly surprised by the variety and ingenuity of such devices to keep people at home even when they are suffering from severe disabilities! Community occupational therapists can be asked to visit and assess the needs, and to apply their skill and knowledge to meeting them.

In addition, enhanced facilities such as sheltered accommodation with warden support for people in their own flat or bungalow in a group is ideal for many, especially if they are on their own. Further provision may take the form of residential accommodation, where each individual has his or her own room but may have meals with other residents, cooked by the home's staff. Such facilities enhance a person's independence, while giving the community support they need and crave.

Human support, too, may be needed. Most general practices in Britain have district or practice nurses attached to them. They are skilled in meeting personal practical needs for medication and dressings, and dealing with physical and emotional issues. Sadly, the increasing demand for their services leaves little time for sitting and listening to people as in the past. For many patients with progressive illnesses, MacMillan or Marie Curie nurses may fill this gap once they have been invited to be involved. Such nurses used to be available solely for people suffering from cancer, but nowadays their value for sufferers from other progressive and incurable conditions has been recognised.

The greatest importance, however, is often the presence of a spouse or carer who is available continually, as Joe was able to be for Mabel. I am often surprised by people's ability to cope with problems – no, challenges – of daily living. But the issue may come when the person is alone at night: 'What happens if. . .?' they ask. Even with a devoted carer such as Joe, the situation may break down, and then. . . what next? They will be glad indeed if the situation has been foreseen and some suitable alternative provision is available. Such provision may be a great help to the carer, too, if he or she becomes tired over time with the burden of caring. A respite break may equip such a carer with the strength to continue their care for another period.

When asked, most people express a wish to live in their own home to the end of their lives. However, people with advancing disease or frailty often do change their minds about their preferred location of care as their needs change.

Hospital

An acute hospital bed   It is one of the enormous strengths of the UK National Health Service that admission to the acute hospital is always available if the acute need arises. Whether we are in our own home, in a hospice or in a nursing home, if there is an acute indication for transfer to hospital for active treatment it is possible to find a bed – somewhere. And there is nowhere better for active or emergency care than with the skills and professional avail-ability in the hospital. But they are noisy places! With the best will in the world, there is always noise – whether of trolleys transferring patients, food trolleys, bells or voices. Nights are disturbed by the arrival of new patients or the calls of confused ones or of those in pain. Then there are the night rounds and the regimentation of timed medicine rounds. I don't need to go on!

Added to all this, there is always pressure on the staff to find a bed for the next admissions for surgery or investigation or emergency care. No, hospital is a welcome place for acute care, but not a place to stay for a longer time.

Intermediate stay   Recently, an initiative has been developed as a stepping-stone between the acute hospital stay and return home. In many ways this is similar to the old convalescent period. It is aimed to reduce 'bed-blocking' in hospital, and to allow for active mobilisation of patients who need preparation for return home. It sounds an excellent idea but its effectiveness will depend on provision of an adequate number of such places or beds, and adequate skilled staff to prepare people for that next move, rather than the place becoming another long-stay home.

Long-term   For some people, long-term care in hospital becomes the best or even the only option. For a variety of reasons, they are too ill or disabled mentally or physically to return home or to be placed in a nursing home. This is an option that has been discouraged over recent decades, where care in the community has been regarded as much better. But for those people, often the elderly, who are in need of continuing medical and nursing care, this may be exactly what is needed. The doctors responsible for the medical care in these units are specialists in their own right, having chosen to specialise in care of the elderly or mental health or another relevant speciality in medicine.

The staff of these units have to keep up to date with progress in medical care, because it is too easy for long-term care wards to be viewed as backwaters. On the other hand they are often staffed by dedicated nurses who have much care, love and experience to share in providing for their patients.

Hospice

The hospice – 'a resting place for travellers' on the journey of life – used to be regarded as the last option for people dying of cancer. Not so any longer! Rather it is a place of skilled medical, nursing and allied professional care where people with a variety of advancing conditions, at any age, may find relief. Hospices are remarkably peaceful places, but also places of fun and laughter, of comfort and care.

Developed, in the modern sense, during the latter half of the twentieth century as a Christian response to pain and suffering, their original work was in the care of individuals, allied with research and education into means of maximising relief from troublesome symptoms. Experience of and demand for their skills spread rapidly throughout the UK and, over the next two decades, throughout the world.

St Christopher's Hospice and St Luke's Home

In 1967, after years of thinking, planning and fundraising, Dr Cicely Saunders realised her ambition to open her own hospice in south London. There she and a team of specially trained doctors, nurses and other professionals could care for people with advanced illnesses including cancer. Her plan was to provide a centre for study of medications and treatments for the symptoms of advanced disease, and so to make the care of people approaching death much more effective. It would be an example and a teaching centre. Cicely had herself trained as a nurse and lady almoner (the modern hospital social worker or care manager) before training as a doctor. She was also a committed Christian, and saw the need for care of whole people: body, mind and spirit. Her previous experience included caring for people at St Luke's Home for the Dying Poor in north London, where she had watched the doctor relieve people's pain with regular administration of morphine by mouth. She herself practised this subsequently at St Joseph's Hospice in east London. This combination of training and experience was to form the basis for St Christopher's Hospice.

At about the same time, and independently, an experienced GP in the north of England opened St Luke's Home in Sheffield, a medical care home very similar to St Christopher's. Professor of General Practice Eric Wilkes was a charismatic figure, who had also seen the need for vastly improved care of patients living with and dying from their illnesses.

These two hospices became the inspiration of a movement that was to spread to some 15 institutions in the UK in the next decade, and then to multiply throughout Britain and to many other countries in the last two decades of the twentieth century. Hospices seemed to mushroom across the world; or, as the Chinese put it, they 'spread like green bamboo shoots in the spring'!

Hospices were charitable institutions, largely funded by charitable giving, and independent of the National Health Service. However, Dr Saunders (later Dame Cicely) tried to ensure that the hospice was closely allied with the NHS, St Christopher's having been opened, as she often said, with a research grant from the Department of Health. The hospice was not to be sidelined, she determined, but would be influential in the care of patients throughout the hospitals and community in the country. However, perhaps even she had not envisaged the extraordinary influence of the hospice movement worldwide!

Although hospices sprang up as a result of local initiatives and as independent services, from an early stage St Christopher's and its Hospice Information Service attempted to encourage siting of hospices appropriately to population density throughout Britain. Others pursued this objective, planning that where possible there should be 25 hospice beds per 100,000 population, then increasing that aim to 40 beds, then 50. To the in-patient units were added home-care teams (an initiative of St Christopher's in 1968), and day-care units (similar to St Luke's in Sheffield). Some years later Douglas MacMillan stimulated the spread of these teams in the community through his MacMillan service, and then spread the idea widely into hospitals as he pump-primed funding for development of hospital palliative-care teams. The work in the community is also served by the Marie Curie nursing service and other charities.

Thanks to these initiatives, most communities in Britain and Ireland are served by trained home-care or MacMillan nurses; have access to a local hospice; and have the benefit of trained palliative-care nurses or teams in the acute hospitals. A speciality has developed within British medicine, known as palliative medicine, with its own training schemes and its own consultant doctors and trained nurses, social workers, counsellors, chaplains and therapists.

But there is still a shortage of palliative-care beds and trained staff, partly because of the very success of, and therefore demand for, the service. Specialist palliative care now sees itself as providing skilled management of pain and difficult symptoms, with the aim of enabling patients to enjoy quality time in their own homes or wherever they would prefer to be. Therefore most hospices operate a short-stay, symptom-management service rather than providing the continuing care of patients from admission to death as, it is popularly thought, used to be the case.

During the two weeks of the average stay of hospice patients, symptoms are controlled as far as is possible and then we encourage people to be up and about in preparation for their return home. Of course, some cannot return home and an appropriate place elsewhere must be sought that will be agreeable to all concerned.

Residential and nursing homes

For people who are unable to return home, long-term nursing care is ideally provided in a nursing home. However, many elderly people do not need nursing care; for them, the security of sheltered accommodation allows the desired level of independence, but with help available when need arises, as we have already seen. Many residential homes are willing to continue to support elderly residents till the end of their lives; but if nursing is needed they may have to move on to the nursing home. There is no reason why

specialist support and advice from the MacMillan or palliative home-care team should not continue to be available in
the nursing homes, and there is considerable benefit from
this sort of co-operation. Nursing home standards have
risen dramatically in recent years, with the emphasis on
adequate-sized single rooms rather than shared rooms, and
the availability of ensuite facilities.

However, this very increase in required standards has
resulted in the closure of other homes and a shortage of
nursing home beds in some parts of the country. Many residential and nursing homes have been established by individual Christians or churches as a response to this need, and
such homes are open to all, regardless of race or creed.

Skills in care

We have looked at the variety of provision of place of care
for people in the late stage of their lives; but equally important is the availability of the skills of care. By this I mean
knowledge of symptom relief, pain management, communication skills, and social and spiritual care. These have
been researched and developed in recent years through the
specialities of elderly care medicine (or geriatrics), palliative
(or hospice) medicine, and pain clinics. Social work, psy-
chology and counselling, hospital and hospice chaplaincies
and bereavement support teams have also sharpened our
understanding of care.

One of the important insights of hospice medicine, and
specifically of Dame Cicely Saunders, was the concept of
'total pain'. She pointed out that people with cancer may
well have physical pain which can be treated with

painkillers such as paracetamol or morphine. But such pain may be allied to emotional pain due to limitation of functions or physical mutilation. Social pain may be part of the problem due to the person's isolation or loneliness or care for dependants. And then there may be spiritual pain expressed; for instance, in a search for meaning in life or assurance about a future. This combination of physical, emotional, social and spiritual pain is not relieved by medication alone; but, in the same way as it is 'total pain', it requires a 'total response' of medicine, listening, communication and caring. Many people will also value prayer! In this way we may aim to enable the person to find their own peace, which will bring true relief from the totality of pain. This can be true of symptoms other than pain; for instance, intractable nausea or breathlessness or depression may also need, and respond to, this total or team care.

Much has been done to enhance relief of pain, and it is believed that almost all people with pain in advanced cancer may have their pain relieved entirely by appropriate use of a combination of analgesics, provided that the elements of total pain are sought and relieved also. Similarly, relief for other symptoms has been researched and much work continues to improve this, particularly by the palliative-care services in the UK and throughout Europe and the world. There is concern, however, that in those countries where euthanasia is acceptable, such pressure for improving and funding research in palliative care tends to dry up.

Such research and improved skills are widely disseminated in medical and specialist publications. Courses and conferences are organised; but there remains a considerable patchiness in such knowledge at the level of the community and of care homes.

We still hear sad stories of people discharged from hospital or hospice who find the provision at home or elsewhere does not match up to what they need and have received. Particularly difficult can be the transition from institution to home or nursing home. Again, the problem may be inadequate communication, or it may be lack of appropriate training. Things have undoubtedly improved, but much still remains to be done, particularly as the expectations of people are raised by experience of the best.

Britain has an increasingly ageing population. Life expectancy is increasing and the percentage of people over the age of 80 continues to rise. With this goes increasing need for the sort of facilities we have talked about here. And care has a price tag attached! So what about the cost of care?

Cost of care

The biggest cost has to be that paid by carers emotionally, socially and personally in providing care for their loved one. This is a care that must continue despite distressing symptoms, disturbed nights and anxious days. It must continue despite the frailty and lack of sense of worth of the person concerned. And it must continue despite the (sometimes repeated) calls for an end to it all. A very big, personal price.

We have referred several times in the previous chapters to this price paid by carers. There needs to be increasing provision for carers themselves to be cared for and to receive physical and financial support. We in the community need to make ourselves aware of the demands such people face, and to find or provide support on a voluntary or statutory basis.

But this section is also concerned with the 'pounds and pence' cost of care. This cost is shared between the community (represented by the Treasury and the NHS), charities and the church (insofar as the church accepts responsibility for providing support) and individual families and carers.

Hospital care and on average about one third of hospice care is funded by the NHS, and so by the Treasury out of general taxation – that is, from you and me by our tax payments. The remaining two thirds or more of hospice care is funded by charitable giving: donations, fundraising events and legacies in the main. It often surprises people that the Health Service contributes so little to hospice care. I refer here to direct funding. In Britain and Ireland a great deal of the work of hospices is performed by volunteers, who save much direct funding by the time and skill they freely give to the hospices.

Residence in nursing and residential homes is largely paid for by the people who use the services. That seems appropriate since they receive accommodation and meals, as well as care and the sense of security, and no longer need to keep up their own homes. For people who are reaching the end of their lives and who need nursing-home care for medical reasons during their last few weeks of life, provision is made for their nursing-home care to be funded by the Health Service, on the grounds that otherwise they would need to occupy a hospital bed.

In some cases accommodation in these homes may be subsidised by churches, and certainly the initial costs of developing homes are sometimes the initiative of the churches, when they recognise a gap in provision.

One way or another, we all have a share in the cost of caring for disabled, frail elderly people and those in the late stage of life who need support.

This was reflected in the House of Lord's Select Committee's report on medical ethics in 1994. It is perhaps instructive that this issue was addressed by the committee which recommended that there should be no change in the law regarding euthanasia, whereas the matter was not addressed at all by the Select Committee which reported in 2005 in support of Lord Joffe's Bill concerning Assisted Dying for the Terminally Ill.

The 1994 report states:

> Despite the inevitable continuing constraints on health-care resources, the rejection of euthanasia as an option for the individual, in the interest of our wider social good, entails a compelling social responsibility to care adequately for those who are elderly, dying or disabled. Such a responsibility is costly to discharge, but is not one which we can afford to neglect. In this connection therefore we make the following recommendations –
>
> • High quality palliative care should be made more widely available by improving public support for the existing hospice movement, ensuring that all general practitioners and hospital doctors have access to specialist advice, and providing more support for relevant training at all levels.
> • Research into new and improved methods of pain relief and symptom control should be adequately supported and the results effectively disseminated.
> • Training of health-care professionals should do more to prepare them for the weighty ethical responsibilities which they carry, by giving greater priority to health-care ethics and counselling and communication skills.

- More formal and regular consideration of health-care ethics at a national level would be helpful.
- Long-term care of those whose disability or dementia makes them dependent should have special regard to the need to maintain the dignity of the individual to the highest possible degree.

We would most strongly agree with all of that.

The world issue again

We started the chapter with reference to Archbishop Desmond Tutu's words concerning the suffering of millions of people around the world living with a terminal illness, who are either unaware of, or unable to access, the care they need. We end the chapter by reflecting back on the vast need of over 50 million people who die each year. As noted earlier, 80% die in the developing world and many have no access to pain control or even the most basic care. It is estimated that 60% would benefit from palliative care.

Help the Hospices is a national charity working hard with three aims:

- To raise awareness of the needs of people living with a terminal illness and their families.
- To increase the availability of hospice and palliative care throughout the world to meet those needs.
- To raise funds for the development of those services, in the UK and around the world.

Surely supporting this is the least we can do.

12

Meaning and Hope

'My flesh came back and I could see again!' Joan was dying. We could all see that. She had been in the hospice ten days and was desperately emaciated, apart from her hugely distended tummy – the seat of her cancer. She ate virtually nothing, drank little, yet never complained. Perhaps that was because she slept most of the time. During those sad days, as they appeared to us, she lost her sight, too. Each day one or other of us went over to see her as she slept to make sure she was still breathing – death was as close as that.

That morning, when I arrived in the hospice, someone asked if I would go and see Joan at once as she had had a bad night and her family were with her. Her son and daughter were sitting with her.

'I'm so sorry you've had a bad night,' I said. 'What happened?'

'It wasn't a bad night,' she replied. 'I slept well till about five o'clock and then I woke up with someone standing by the bed. "You must come with me, Joan," he said.

'My flesh came back and I could see again, and I said to him, "Yes, Lord, but could I say goodbye to my son and daughter?"'

'He said, "Yes, but then you must come."'

'So I asked the nurses to send for my family – and here they are,' she said, as though to assure me that what she had said was true. She made no reference to the fact that, physically, we could see no difference. But, spiritually, she was healed.

The next thing she did was to send for her minister (the local Methodist minister), 'to help me be sure I'm ready to go with him'. Two days later she died, or, as she would put it, went with him, her Lord Jesus.

Meaning and hope

Shortly after the Second World War a very powerful book was published in Austria by a Jewish psychiatrist who had survived three years in German concentration camps. Dr Viktor Frankl's book was translated and published in English in 1953 and re-published (with an extended section) in 1967 as *Man's Search for Meaning*.

Dr Frankl argues that man desperately needs a sense of meaning for life, and a goal to live for. During the years in the concentration camps, he and the other prisoners lost everything – possessions and clothing went at reception, along with any moveable item, even their hair (every last hair on their bodies!). They lost their previous identity, their achievements, even their name. They lost their accustomed food, their health. The one thing they had to cling on to was hope. And when a man lost his hope the end for him was very close. He comments, 'It is a peculiarity of man that he can only live by looking to the future . . . And this is his salvation in the most difficult moments of his existence, although he sometimes has to force his mind to the task.'

Patients have sometimes reminded me of that. David, for example, was admitted with an advanced and incurable cancer of the lung. He was very ill. But it was November and there was a birthday coming at the beginning of December. 'Shall I live to see my birthday, doc?' Yes, I thought so.

After the birthday had been successfully achieved, 'Shall I live to see Christmas?' It seemed possible, and so it happened.

New Year would be less of an event, but it was something to be reached for, and he made it.

Now what? Easter was a very long way away, and, frankly, did not seem likely for David. For three weeks or so David seemed to become less well. Then someone suggested a painting-by-numbers set. David took to it and produced a very creditable first effort at painting, something he had never done before. Another outline was attractively filled, then David said he wanted to try painting his own picture – with a very good result. Now he was on his way; every day saw him at work on the next picture.

He found a competition for disabled artists. 'I'm disabled, if anyone is,' he said. He designed and painted his own picture for the competition – and won! During the next weeks David filled his room with completed or part-completed pictures. 'This one's for my son, this one for my brother. . .' He painted far into the night.

Some weeks later he failed to wake at the usual time, and died very peacefully an hour or so later. That day his wife said to me that in that last month or two he had painted pictures for every one of his family and relatives. The last one was drying in his room as we spoke. 'Yes,' said one of the nurses, 'and he stayed painting that till two o'clock this morning, as though he knew he had that much time left to complete it!'

David's life had become filled with a new sort of purpose and achievement. Frankl again: 'Those who knew that there was a task waiting for them to fulfil were most apt to survive.'

Frankl's book emphasises the importance of a sense of meaning in life. When a group of fellow-prisoners were on the point of giving up hope, he had been asked to provide encouragement. 'God knows,' he writes, 'I was not in the mood to give psychological explanations or to preach any sermons – to offer my comrades a kind of medical care for their souls. I was cold and hungry, irritable and tired, but I had to make the effort and use this unique opportunity.'

He tried to set their situation in context – their past, their losses, even the hopes for change, their suffering. Even under such circumstances (for many, a fourth or fifth winter in a Second World War concentration camp):

Life never ceases to have a meaning, and this infinite meaning of life includes suffering and dying, privation and death. I asked the poor creatures who listened attentively to me in the darkness of the hut to face up to the seriousness of our position. They must not lose hope but should keep their courage in the certainty that the hopelessness of our struggle did not detract from dignity and meaning. I said that someone looks down on each of us in difficult hours – a friend, a wife, someone alive or dead, or a God – and he would not expect us to disappoint him. He would hope to find us suffering proudly – not miserably – knowing how to die.[1]

In our case, too, we search for meaning, and in this chapter – and book – I want to underline the need for hope. Meaning encompasses past and present and sets a context for a future; but, as David found, hope, where it is more than wishful thinking, helps to fill that future with expectation.

But that is the rub: 'more than wishful thinking'.

Patients suffering from cancer are used to wishful thinking, expressed in the encouraging noises many hear frequently: 'You'll be all right in the end; illness often gets worse before it gets better.' But they know that this illness is not going to get better. Hope that is impossible is not hope!

Hence comes our encouragement to doctors and relatives dealing with such patients to tell them the truth, but to be supportive with it. After all, there is so much that we can do these days to relieve pain and suffering and to allow life to be as full and worthwhile as possible to the last stages. So we need to offer realistic hope to strengthen the sufferer to cope with this stage, too.

The modern disease – hopelessness

Hopelessness is, of course, the modern disease. We are told that the majority of patients who visit their GP these days are suffering from depression. Indeed, anyone listening to the news broadcasts or reading their newspaper could be forgiven for feeling depressed about the state of the world! We have suggested that despair is one of the thoughts that may lead a person to suicide. But this feeling of depression, sometimes allied with 'unattached anxiety', is often not a response to circumstances (reactive depression) but a settled attitude of mind.

Here is one of the weaknesses of existentialism. If this life is all there is, and my personal sense of well-being is the final good, then why should I not be depressed and despairing when life is so often unfair and uninviting? Particularly so, if I have received news of an incurable and life-threatening disease.

Our world calls out for a realistic hope and hopefulness.

Terminal illness?

Ultimately, however, what hope can we offer in terminal illness?

So far in this book we have tried to avoid that term, although it is widely used in advanced cancer. So we ought to face it.

The phrase 'terminal illness' has three problems with its use. First, it is so imprecise as to be disturbing. When does an illness become terminal? Does that happen when it is recognised to be incurable? Sometimes that may be months, even years, before the date of death, even with the 'normal' rate of progress of the illness. In other instances, circumstances may change; there may be unexpected remission, realisation of a mistaken diagnosis, even a miraculous cure. So that 'terminal' may be entirely wrong. Or does it start at a set period before death? Our problem with that is that the date of death is not clearly defined in advance! Or is it when a particular stage in the symptoms of the illness is reached? Even that is not easily defined.

Secondly, it is so hope-destroying. 'I know I'm terminal,' I sometimes hear people say. Life already feels as though it has passed them by. 'But how do you feel at present?' I ask.

'Oh, reasonably well, only weaker, perhaps.' So there is still life to be lived. Sometimes I used to add, 'I ride a motor-bike. They are said to be dangerous: my life may be shorter than yours! But each day is to be lived. How can we make yours better today?'

The third problem is particularly for the Christian: to what station are we travelling in life? The terminus? No; for us death is the great Change-Station! 'All change!' Jesus assures us that the next part of the journey is far more glorious than even the best of this part (John 14:2–4). There is a great certainty open to us, and that is the Christian hope, to which we may now turn.

The Christian hope

The assurance for our future begins with an experience in the present time. Whatever our physical age, and however near to death we may be, God's promise is that 'to all who received him [Jesus], who believed in his name, he gave the right to become children of God' (John 1:12). In Chapter 6 we spoke about a senior nurse who came to the hospice for her last few days of life. She found this newness of life as her present experience three days before her death, and what a difference it made!

It does, or should, make an enormous difference. Even though the body's weakness and symptoms may progress, yet the internal life continues to develop. Paul says that:

Though outwardly we are wasting away, yet inwardly we are being renewed day by day. For our light and momentary troubles are achieving for us an eternal glory that far outweighs them all. So we fix our eyes not on what is seen, but on what is unseen. For what is seen is temporary, but what is unseen is eternal. (2 Corinthians 4:16–18)

It is almost as though he knew what we are going through!

Eric shared that experience of the present hope. He was a church organist and a deeply committed Christian. He was nevertheless shocked at the diagnosis of inoperable cancer. Through various treatments his faith stood him in good stead, but nights became long and restless. One night his wife wakened to find Eric seated on the edge of the bed holding his head in his hands. 'What are you doing, Eric?' she asked.

'Just thinking,' he said.

'What about, Eric?' she asked.

'About death,' he replied.

'What about it?'

'It's just blackness and nothingness,' he said.

'Oh, Eric.' And she held him in the darkness.

Some three weeks later I met him as an ambulance brought him into the hospice.

'I'm sorry that you have been feeling so low,' I said.

'Oh, not now,' he replied. 'I'm covered over with the peace of God like a warm blanket!'

A future certainty

Not only are we assured of a present experience of peace, but there is a future certainty to be expected. We referred to Jesus' promise for us; one reference to it is in John's Gospel, chapter 14. He promises to take us to himself, though not necessarily in the same dramatic way that Joan experienced, as recorded at the beginning of this chapter. Jesus says:

> 'Do not let your hearts be troubled. Trust in God; trust also in me. In my Father's house are many rooms; if it were not so, I would have told you. I am going there to prepare a place for you. And if I go and prepare a place for you, I will come back and take you to be with me that you also may be where I am. You know the way to the place where I am going.'
>
> Thomas said to him, 'Lord, we don't know where you are going, so how can we know the way?'
>
> Jesus answered, 'I am the way and the truth and the life. No-one comes to the Father except through me.' (John 14:1–6)

A definition of Christian hope

Christian hope has been defined as a certain assurance of things not yet experienced. I like the definiteness of that. It is so different from wishful thinking about the future! This assurance rests on the definite promises of Scripture. We have Jesus' own words – and the whole of John 14 to 17 is relevant.

But, you may ask, 'How certain is that?'

In times of uncertainty or doubt, I find I go back to the certainty of Jesus' life, death and resurrection. Here is the basis for our Christian hope. We need have no doubt about his life: it is widely attested in writings by historians of the time. Jesus' crucifixion, too, is not a point of dispute. And the resurrection? Well, our entire Christian faith rests on the fact that Jesus rose from the dead, was seen over a period of 40 days by many different witnesses, and later appeared to Saul on the Damascus road. Paul lists the witnesses for us in 1 Corinthians 15.

> For what I received I passed on to you as of first importance:
> that Christ died for our sins according to the Scriptures, that he
> was buried, that he was raised on the third day according to
> the Scriptures, and that he appeared to Peter, and then to the
> Twelve. After that, he appeared to more than five hundred of
> the brothers at the same time, most of whom are still living,
> though some have fallen asleep. Then he appeared to James,
> then to all the apostles, and last of all he appeared to me also,
> as to one abnormally born.
>
> For I am the least of the apostles and do not even deserve to
> be called an apostle, because I persecuted the church of God.
> But by the grace of God I am what I am, and his grace to me
> was not without effect. (1 Corinthians 15:3–10)

People have identified that if Jesus is not risen from the
dead, then our faith has no basis in fact. But attempts to
discredit the evidence of Scripture have failed – see, for
example, Frank Morison's *Who Moved the Stone?* Or Josh
McDowell's *More Than a Carpenter*. No, we can rest assured
that Jesus rose from the dead. If so, we can also rest on what
he said of himself, his relation to God the Father, and on his
promises to his followers.

We rest, then, on the certainty that at death we go to be
with him – as he said to the dying thief on the cross beside
his: 'Today you will be with me in paradise' (Luke 23:43).

Unless, of course, he returns in glory first. And for that, too,
we have his own promise in Matthew 24:30 (and elsewhere):

> They will see the Son of Man coming on the clouds of the sky,
> with power and great glory. And he will send his angels with a
> loud trumpet call, and they will gather his elect from the four
> winds, from one end of the heavens to the other. (Matthew
> 24:30–31)

It is reinforced by the angelic visitors who stood with the disciples at the time when Jesus ascended into heaven, 40 days after his resurrection, in full view of the watching disciples. Luke records for us in Acts 1 that:

> . . . suddenly two men dressed in white stood beside them [the disciples]. 'Men of Galilee,' they said, 'why do you stand here looking into the sky? This same Jesus, who has been taken from you into heaven, will come back in the same way you have seen him go into heaven.' (Acts 1:10–11)

This promise is unwrapped further for us by Paul in 1 Thessalonians 4, where he relates it particularly to those who grieve after the death of loved ones, and in view of uncertainty as to whether they will ever see them again.

> Brothers, we do not want you to be ignorant about those who fall asleep, or to grieve like the rest of men, who have no hope. We believe that Jesus died and rose again and so we believe that God will bring with Jesus those who have fallen asleep in him. According to the Lord's own word, we tell you that we who are still alive, who are left till the coming of the Lord, will certainly not precede those who have fallen asleep. For the Lord himself will come down from heaven, with a loud command, with the voice of the archangel and with the trumpet call of God, and the dead in Christ will rise first. After that, we who are still alive and are left will be caught up together with them in the clouds to meet the Lord in the air. And so we will be with the Lord for ever. Therefore encourage one another with these words. (1 Thessalonians 4:13–18)

You will notice that in verse 17 the promise is that we who are left will be caught up together with them in the clouds – what reassurance that at death neither we nor our loved ones are lost and gone for ever, if we and they have died in faith in Jesus! But the climax is not that we shall be with them for ever, but that 'we will be with the Lord for ever'.

And that brings us to one further promise of Scripture, this time in the Revelation. John tells us of a new heaven and a new earth, and of a glorious ultimate future. He hears a great declaration:

> Now the dwelling of God is with men, and he will live with them. They will be his people and God himself will be with them and be their God. He will wipe every tear from their eyes. There will be no more death or mourning or crying or pain, for the old order of things has passed away. (Revelation 21:3–4)

Of course there are questions that need to be answered to the best of our ability. But we have a certainty to secure our hearts.

And that security, that ultimate assurance that God does know us, our needs, our difficulties and our questions encourages us to ask another. In the light of God's care of our eternity, should we not trust him with our last months, weeks, days?

The psalmist said:

> . . . I trust in you, O Lord;
> I say, 'You are my God.'
> My times are in your hands;
>   deliver me from my enemies
>   and from those who pursue me.
> Let your face shine on your servant;
>   save me in your unfailing love.
>   (Psalm 31:14–16)

Let us leave our times in his hands, and be thankful.

Epilogue: Decision Time

So we come to the end of our exploration of the issues surrounding euthanasia and physician-assisted suicide. It is decision time.

In the United Kingdom

Four decades of discussion in the United Kingdom around the question of euthanasia led to the setting up of a Select Committee of the House of Lords in 1994. Their remit was to look at medical ethical issues at the end of life and to advise the House. They produced a carefully reasoned report after receiving and reading much submitted evidence, hearing verbal testimony and visiting the Netherlands to see the effect of the relaxation of attitudes at that stage. They recommended that there be no change in the law. This was strongly supported in subsequent discussion in both Houses of Parliament.

A decision had been made.

Over the last ten years the issues have not gone away. A further Select Committee was established by the House of Lords in 2004 specifically to examine and report on a drafted Bill known as the 'Assisted Dying for the Terminally Ill' Bill. They also sought evidence very widely, as the former committee had. They visited the State of Oregon, the Netherlands and Switzerland to enquire about practice under the legislation in these countries. They, too, produced a detailed report and recommended discussion in parliament. They made recommendations about refinement of the proposed Bill.

So the national debate has been informed and encouraged. If you have been interested over the years, you will have heard or read evidence being put by many medical and legal groups and by pressure groups advocating either change or no change in the law. This has led to parliamentary debate and to decision about legislation. Our representatives in parliament will need to decide.

Factors for our own decisions

In this book we have looked at arguments for and against euthanasia and I hope that we have seen some of the issues more clearly. Let me summarise the factors we need to weigh as Christians in coming to our decision about euthanasia or assisted dying.

Is it necessary?

For most people, good modern medicine illuminated by the research and skills of palliative care enables effective control of symptoms and renders euthanasia unnecessary. Supportive care by relatives, nurses, doctors and carers can maintain and improve the hope, dignity and worth of the individual to the end.

Would it be threatening?

For elderly frail people, for disabled people and for handicapped infants, legalisation of euthanasia might constitute a threat. The economic arguments and the cost of caring, as well as the pressure that some of these people would inevitably face, would make it dangerous and potentially threatening.

Will it provide control?

The evidence of countries where euthanasia has been legalised does not support the view that it controls misuse. Involuntary and non-voluntary euthanasia continue unabated, but there is also recurrent pressure to extend the conditions for which killing people can be justified.

Would it alter doctors' practice?

There are dangers in extending a doctor's role from caring to killing. It will alter the doctor–patient relationship, and there are some professionals, few though they may be, to whom this right would become addictive. Dr Harold Shipman got away with murder, literally, for decades!

What about God's commandment?

Ultimately, we have a specific prohibition in the sixth of the Ten Commandments, and we have seen that these were not abrogated by the Lord Jesus. His teaching, example and suffering are our final sanction.

Implications of a decision against euthanasia

Such a decision comes at a price. If we agree that euthanasia is not our way, we need to support the alternatives for people with a fatal illness or with loss of hope. They need our help and care.

Palliative care

Specialist palliative care needs to be very widely – more widely – available. There must be improved application of communication skills and insights; medications for pain control and symptom relief; and support for carers in all hospitals, in the community and in our residential institutions.

Nursing-home care

Good as many nursing homes are, staff need better training in palliative nursing skills and the use of techniques that are practised in the hospices. We need better liaison between hospice, hospital and nursing home, so that on transfer patients do not suffer from lack of knowledge of how they have been cared for, or lack of medicines or apparatus.

Hospice beds

In some areas of the country there is good provision of hospice beds; in other areas there are waiting lists that are too long. Many people who need a hospice bed are unlikely to be able to wait weeks on a waiting list! On the other hand, an inflexible two-week rule is distressing and unkind. Very ill people need to continue to be cared for in their hospice bed for as long as it takes.

And yet it is not kind, either, to keep people lingering in an environment where others are dying after a short period. There needs to be provision for people who are going to need the skills of palliative care for weeks or even months. Perhaps the answer is to have 'intermediate stay' hospice-type beds in a nursing home wing attached to the hospice or in a designated nursing home staffed by palliative care staff.

Widened palliative-care training

Many specialist palliative-care teams are involved in training and this needs to be increasingly available to, and encouraged for, doctors and nurses of all specialities, for nursing home staff, for volunteers and for the community at large.

Personal decision time

Some of us may have to face these issues on a professional basis: how will we respond to requests from one or other of our patients or their relatives if euthanasia or assisted suicide should be made legal? And how will we respond to subsequent discussions in our professional societies whether or not the law is changed?

Others of us may have a more personal choice to make. You may have to listen to the pleas of a loved relative, or perhaps even have to make your own decision about the end of life. It is wise to have faced these matters beforehand, and to have settled how you balance the arguments when they can be viewed dispassionately. At this time we can come to our own decision without the pressure of personal emotions affecting it.

Of course, the decision will need to be reviewed if our own, or our loved one's, circumstances change, but even then it will have helped to have settled our position – as Christians – before the Lord.

Yes, this book has been written specifically for Christians. My hope is that it will help us make our decisions with a better understanding of the issues. My prayer is that you will make your decisions in the light of our loving Lord who is the Way, the Truth and the Life.

Let us allow Dr John Caroe to help us with a final meditation, in a poem he has written especially for this book.

A song of the dying

'I AM' here?
Now? Straddling eternity?
Now is the conjunction approaching,
Eternity and destiny, in marriage with my frailty.
Here is the consummation of my journey.
Here I am.

Hear 'I AM'
In the beauty of my mind.
Wires may rust and contacts break without,
But the exquisite, enigmatic coding of my circuits
Still testify within to the genius of my maker.
His heart still swells with ecstasy of creation
And in that heart I thus exist.
Here I am.

Hear 'I AM'
In the beauty of my flesh.
Skin may rot and sphincters leak,
But each organ still gives thunderous praise
To the genius of my creator,
Whose heart still swells
With the ecstasy of my being,
And in anticipation of that reunion
That translates 'Death' to 'Life',
And relocates my soul to Paradise.

Attend, my friend, my hallowed transformation.
Hear 'I AM', for here am I.

Notes

Chapter 3

1. Select Committee on the Assisted Dying for the Terminally Ill Bill, Vol. 1: Report, The Stationery Office, London, 2005.
2. Billet d'Etat, a Report for the Policy Council – Voluntary Euthanasia, Royal Court House, Guernsey, 2004.
3. Van der Maas, P.J., van Delden, J.J.M., Pijnenborg, L., Looman, C.W.N. 'Euthanasia and other medical decisions concerning the end of life', *The Lancet*, 1991; 338; 669–674.
4. Onwuteaka-Philipsen, B.D. et al. 'Euthanasia and other end of life decisions in the Netherlands in 1990, 1995, and 2001', *The Lancet*, 2003.
5. Van der Heide et al. (on behalf of the EURELD Consortium). 'End of life decision-making in six European countries: descriptive study', *The Lancet*, 2003; 361; 345–350.
6. This section is based on text from www.islamatschool.org.uk/GC/GCSETopicsPages/Euthanasia.htm, and quotes extensively from it.
7. Hathout, Hassan, MD, PhD www.asca/updates/2–2/14ahtm
8. Gordon, Dr Harvey. *Q&A about Jewish Tradition and Issue of Assisted Death 1998.* Quoted in Reform Judaism online, Fall 2005 http://reformjudaismmag.org/Articles/Index.cfm?id=1049
9. Central Conference of American Rabbis Responsum, 1989. Quoted in Reform Judaism online, fall (ibid.).

10. Rabbi Richard F. Address (ed.), *A Time to Prepare* (revised edn, 2002), UAHC Press, New York, p. 42. Quoted in Reform Judaism online/ 2005 fall (ibid.)

11. www.bbc.co.uk/religion/ethics/euthanasia/hindu.shtml

12. Rinpoche, Lama Zopa, Advice and Practices for Death and Dying for the Benefit of self and others, FPMT, 2003, p. 40.

13. Campbell, Courtney, S. (Professor of Philosophy, Oregon State University, USA) *Euthanasia and Religion*. The UNESCO courier 2000–01.www.unesco.org/courier/2000_01/uk/ethique/txt1.html

14. Williams, Dr Rowan (Archbishop of Canterbury), 'The gifts reserved for age: perceptions of the elderly', *Church Times*, 6 September 2005.

Chapter 5

1. Wyatt, J., *Matters of Life and Death*, InterVarsity Press, 1998.

Chapter 7

1. Lloyd Carr, G., *After the Storm: Hope in the Wake of Suicide*, IVP, 1990.

2. See, for example, Samson (Judges 16:23–31), Saul (1 Samuel 31:1–6; 2 Samuel 1:23); even Judas (Matthew 27:5; Acts 1:16–20) whose disaster is not his suicide but his betrayal of Jesus.

3. Select Committee for the Assisted Dying for the Terminally Ill Bill. Vol.1, Report. The Stationery Office, London, 2005.

4. Nightingale Alliance, *Potential Dangers of Physician-Assisted Suicide and Euthanasia*, www.nightingalealliance.org/cgi-bin/home.pl?article=96

5. Groenewoud J.H. et al., 'Clinical Problems with the Performance of Euthanasia and Physician-Assisted Suicide in the Netherlands', in *New England Journal of Medicine* 2000, 342:551–56.

Chapter 9

1. 'Withholding and Withdrawing Life-prolonging Treatments: Good Practice in Decision-making', General Medical Council, 2002.

Prayers, Promises and Prescriptions for Healing

by Paul Kraus

'I recommend this lovely book, which will bring hope and comfort to anyone facing serious illness.'

Fiona Castle

Some years ago Paul Kraus was given only months to live. Forced to re-evaluate his life, he discovered the miraculous in every day, going on to write several books for cancer sufferers and others facing any kind of illness or 'life sentence'.

In this volume he brings together the wisdom of the ages, interwoven with his own spiritual journey. These prayers, meditations, poems and affirmations are easy to read, and address our need for healing at all levels: body, mind, spirit and emotions.

All of us have the potential to experience the power of God within us. My hope is that this collection of prayers, scriptures and biblical affirmations on healing will not only help people in difficulties on their life journey but will also encourage readers to focus on life's ultimate meaning and purpose.

Paul Kraus

2. Dyer, C., 'Court rules in favour of GMC's guidance on withholding treatment', *British Medical Journal* 2005; 331, 309.

Chapter 10

1. From *BMA News Review*, April 1995.

Chapter 12

1. Frankl, Viktor, *Man's Search for Meaning*, Hodder and Stoughton, 1987.